CW00505229

Overleaf: A print from an original painting by Isaac Mendes Bellisario (1795-1849)

Beautiful JAMAICA

JAMAICA 50 EDITION

LMH PUBLISHING LIMITED

10 9 8 7 6 5 4 3 2 1

Editorial Team: Kenisha T. Duff, Tony Patel, K. Sean Harris & Mike Henry
Cover design: Sanya Dockery
Main front cover photograph: Kimanee Wilson, Pulse Supermodel
Typeset & book layout: Sanya Dockery

Published by: LMH Publishing Limited
Suite 10-11
Sagicor Industrial Park
7 Norman Road
Kingston C.S.O., Jamaica
Tel.: (876) 938-0005; Fax: (876) 759-8752
Email: lmhbookpublishing@cwjamaica.com
Website: www.lmhpublishing.com

Printed in China ISBN: 978-976-8245-00-7

NATIONAL LIBRARY OF JAMAICA CATALOGUING IN PUBLICATION DATA

Blake, Evon
Beautiful Jamaica : Jamaica 50 edition / Evon Blake
8th ed.
p. : ill. (some col.) ; cm
ISBN 978-976-8245-00-7

1. Jamaica – Description and travel – 21st century
917.292 dc 22

Jamaica

I saw my land in the morning
And oh, but she was fair
The hills flamed upwards scorning
Death and failure here.

I saw through the mists of morning
A wave like a sea set free
Faith to the dawn returning
Dark tide bright unity.

I saw my friends in the morning
They called from an equal gate
"Build now: whilst time is burning
Forward before it's late."

The Old Gods awake.
Past and Future break
On as the voices roll
Move as a single whole
Forward
Forward
Forward
Oh country to your goal.

Michael Garfield Smith

ACKNOWLEDGEMENTS

We would like to offer our gratitude and thanks to everyone who assisted in making this, the Jamaica 50 Edition of Beautiful Jamaica, a resounding success.

Businesses: Susie's Bakery; Tracks & Records; South Beach Cafe; Black River Safari; Ian Flemming Airport; Headline Entertainment; Pulse Modeling Agency; National Gallery of Jamaica; YS Falls; Scotchies Jerk Centre; Spanish Court Hotel; Bob Marley Museum; The Hope Botanical Gardens; Praise Academy of Dance; Jamaica Netball Assoication; Dolphin Cove.

Jamaica Information Service (JIS): photographs in Parade of Prime Ministers and Heads of State (Sir Kenneth Blackburn the only exception).

People: Mr. & Mrs. Tony Patel; Sophia Max-Brown; Her Excellency Lady Allen; Senator Marlene Malahoo Forte; Ian Wilkinson; Kay Osborne; Kenneth Benjamin; Patrice Wilson-McHugh; Wayne Chen; Lascelles Chin; Donna Duncan-Scott; Abraham Mandara; Jerome Hamilton; Kingsley Cooper; Dr. Henry Lowe; Lisa Henry; Noel Hyton; Colin Lesle; Racquel Jones; Captain Basil Jarrett.

Photographers: Roy Sweetland; Stuart Reeves; Donnette Zacca; Tony Patel; Amanda Gibson; Robert Davis; Reginald Allen.

CONTENTS

FLASHBACK 2
HISTORICAL SNAP SHOTS 6
NATIONAL EMBLEMS 12
NATIONAL HEROES 16
GOVERNANCE 20
PARADE OF PRIME MINISTERS 28
HEADS OF STATE 36
LAW & ORDER 40
ARCHITECTURE 46
HISTORICAL TOWNS 54
FACES OF JAMAICA 62
RELIGION 72
EDUCATION 80
WOMEN: THE FAMOUS, THE BEAUTEOUS & THE FABULOUS 88
ARTS & ENTERTAINMENT 100
NATION AT PLAY 110
TOURISM 118
PARKS & BOTANICAL GARDENS 132
JAMAICAN COCKTAILS & CUISINES 140
PATOIS & THINGS JAMAICAN 148
KINGSTON: JEWEL OF THE CARIBBEAN 152
FRONTLINERS 160
HEALTH 174
INDUSTRY 180
JAMAICA: PLACE TO INVEST 188
JAMAICA 50 & BEYOND 198

EVON BLAKE
Author & Originator
1906 - 1988

The late author and publisher Evon Blake was a successful full-time, professional journalist for 45 years. His career was studded with noteworthy firsts and events, some of which are:

- *The first native writer to be given a Gleaner front page byline (1938).*
- *The first writer to be chosen by the Government (1951) to represent the Jamaican Press at the Festival of Britain.*
- *'The Best of Evon Blake', a 104-page compilation of some of his most controversial Gleaner columns, was published in 1968 and sold 2000 copies in a month –a Jamaican record – and is now a collector's item.*
- *In 1974, he was made a Commander of the Order of Distinction, the first such honour to a Jamaican journalist.*

As owners of the copyright of this book, we carry on, in this the Jamaica 50 Edition, Evon's vision of presenting Jamaica in a manner worthy of a country that Evon eloquently described as thus: "There's no place on earth as lovely as Jamaica, no people more wonderful and hospitable than Jamaicans. Jamaica is God's little country."

FLASHBACK

As we pass the milestone of 'Jamaica 50' those of us; like myself must be given the benefit of indulging ourselves especially as we have lived the 50 years and beyond and would have had the benefit of first hand knowledge of what it was really like to be around back then, and where we are coming from.

It gives us the benefit of hindsight and in many cases sets the juices flowing. For my part there are many parallels between the life of the book 'Beautiful Jamaica' it's author, Evon Blake and Jamaica's fight for Independence; and the challenges they (the Country and Evon Blake the author) faced.

For one must realize that the commanding heights of an economy are invariably controlled or directed by the image makers and the opinion formers. A world where those of the then 'plantocracy' felt none but the privileged must enter.

In the early history of the communications world it was the printed word; newspapers, books and radio that played these roles. And these modes of communication were never to be owned by blacks nor advocated by blacks; and indeed Jamaica was no different from the rest of the world.

Thus to be attracted to or wishing to be a publisher in those days required a pioneering spirit and a deep sense of belief in one's self and an urge and drive to succeed without losing one's identity and focus; this challenge would even be more daunting as it required the Capital and Money which were constantly denied to

Top left to right: (then) Sandals Dunns River; an aluminum plant
Bottom: A graduation ceremony at the University of the West Indies

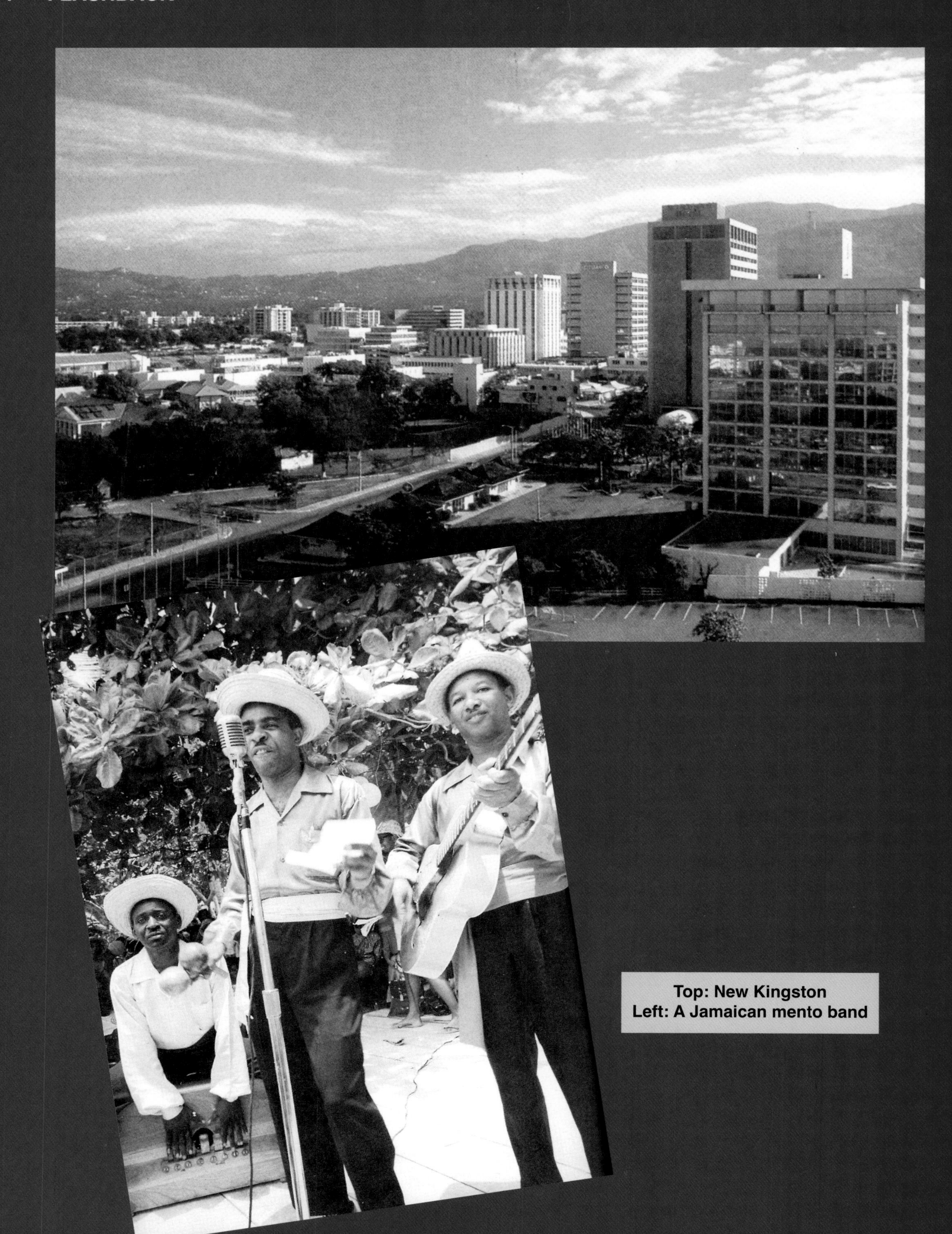

Top: New Kingston
Left: A Jamaican mento band

Evon and those of his colour. This is perhaps what inspired Evon on that historic day when he disrobed and dove into the swimming pool at the then elitist Myrtle Bank Hotel; causing all the whites and mulattoes to flee from the pool.

Jim Crow existed in Jamaica well into the sixties.

For despite Evon's unchallengeable skill and acumen as a journalist and his renowned grasp of the English Language, matched only by his imposing stature and integrity in business ; he had to use creative ways to meet his publishing aims and aspirations.

All of this, however, were considered as mere challenges to Evon and he surmounted them all, defeating the Status Quo' at both the racial and economic level; for, not being satisfied with writing for the white owned newspaper, he formed his own publishing company and published the Spotlight magazine; out of which emerged many a renowned columnist and writer. Seeing the need to expand his horizon and writing skills and satisfying his need and urge to write about us as we are and not as people see us; he decided that as a proud Jamaican he should record the story of a beautiful country through his expert eyes of an author and self publisher. And so using a unique approach; one rooted in the social, physical and historical structure of the country; using people, places and things, he captured the story of Jamaica and its achievements, befitting its motto: Out of Many One People.

For the front cover he chose the beauty of Jamaican women; many of whom conquered the world's Beauty Pageants and for the back cover the scenes of flora, fauna and places.

He used his creative skills to include the Giants of Industry knowing full well they and their companies needed and required this kind of gift book to reflect the pride in their companies and country. Needing then to find the capital to print this high cost book about Jamaica, Evon realized it could only be produced by selling advertising space and pre-selling copies as gifts to these business czars and to the Government for Ministers and Ministries to give to their counterparts.

For in those days many were the embarrassing moments when on visiting or being visited one had nothing of world class standard to give.

Thus it might be said that Evon's Beautiful Jamaica was Jamaica's first coffee table gift book. Eight editions and five reprints would probably make it also one of the most widely read Jamaican publications.

And one deserving of taking its rightful pride of place in the annals of Jamaican self published publications.

To Evon and his creative genius.

MIKE HENRY
Publisher

HISTORICAL SNAPSHOTS

Water Wheel at Tryall, Hanover

Sligoville Great House, St. Catherine

Fort Charles, Port Royal

Negril Light House, Westmoreland

Nature and human hands have combined to create in Jamaica many landmarks that will endure for centuries to come, perhaps forever.

Those that are Nature's creation tell the story of great earthquakes which reduced mountains to rubble and diverted rivers, leaving only stones as a geological chart for the courses they once followed.

Sea shells and marine fossils lie embedded in the spectacular Nonsuch Caves of Portland, 300 feet above sea level. Not only do they attract foreign and local curiousity, but they pose interesting questions for scientists, who have also discovered volcanic rock all along the mountain slopes and seashore of north-eastern Jamaica.

Of man-made landmarks there is no shortage. Old forts and their once powerful cannon; stonewalls and castles overgrown with foliage; great iron wheels that were a part of the hundreds of estates which dotted the island in the era of sugar and slavery. Perilously winding roads through the mountains bespeak the genius of British engineers and the sweat, blood and toil of African slaves.

Since independence, it has been realized that these are part of the national heritage, which should be preserved. With its limited budget the Jamaica National Heritage Trust does what it can, conscious of the fact that each succeeding generation must have its share of discovery, pay its own share of the bill and experience its own thrill of interpreting the present through the relics of the past.

The Spanish Era

Spanish occupation of Jamaica (1494–1655) added only two significant paragraphs to its history: forced into slavery, the indigenous Taino population was wiped out, and the first African slaves imported to replace them.

Columbus' son Diego, built the first town and spent his longest sojourn at Sevilla La Neuva, on flatlands near St. Ann's Bay where the explorer first landed from his flagship, the Santa Maria.

Plagued by malaria, the colonists later abandoned Sevilla La Neuva and trekked overland to establish St. Jago de la Vega (today's Spanish Town) on the dry south-coast plain of St. Catherine, within view of Kingston harbour and the Palisadoes. This was abandoned with less than token resistance when the English fleet showed up in 1655.

Back over the mountains they fled, to the north-coast, then by boat to Cuba. To continue their fighting, they left behind a loose guerilla force consisting largley of their freed slaves and runaway Coromantees, who were later to become famous as the Maroons, led by Christoval Arnaldo de Ysasi. The English changed the name St. Jago de le Vega to Spanish Town and made it their capital.

Much of the glory has faded, but the town remains, its historic square flanked by the well-preserved shell of the Old King's House, the Old House of Assembly, the now burnt out Court House and the Rodney Memorial.

The Spanish also built the costal towns of Montego Bay, Port Antonio, Port Maria, Oracabessa (Golden Head) and Ocho Rios. More Spanish echoes are heard in the names of mountains, villages and rivers: Mount Diablo, Puerto Seco, Rio Beuno, Rio Cobre and of course, the majestic Rio Grande, which offers the unique Jamaican attraction of rafting.

Columbus Park, St.Ann

The English Era

English settlers developed sugar with slave labour, whilst maintaining a form of self-government, which suited both themselves and England.

After years of waging a losing guerilla war with the Maroons, they signed a peace treaty, then proceeded to undermine it by whittling away the freedoms it guaranteed. Religious and economic pressure in England forced Queen Victoria to free the slaves in 1838. The planters were paid for their loss but, deprived of forced labour, plantations went bankrupt by the hundreds.

Pressure for land and rights of freedom by the fast multiplying ex-slave population, had no effect on the Jamaican House of Assembly or the British Parliament. Finally, in 1865, at Morant Bay in the eastern parish of St. Thomas, they formed a protest march, and in the ensuing clash with the armed volunteer force in the parish, the Custos (a local official representing the governor) was killed along with several other whites.

Declaring it a rebellion, Governor Edward John Eyre reacted with a savagery, equalled only by early American generals sent to quell Indian uprisings. Proclaiming marital law, Eyre turned the trigger-happy militia loose on the "rebels" with an apalling score of casualities; 469 hanged or shot willy-nilly; 600-including pregnant women – flogged; over 1,000 men, women, and children wounded, and as many black homes and villages burnt to the ground. Among those hanged were ex-slave, Paul Bogle, and a "free colored" assemblyman, George William Gordon. Gordon, whose warnings of trouble to come if the peasants were not given land, was named as leader of the conspiracy, though there was no evidence against him. Together with Bogle, he was deemed responsible for the "rebellion" and they were branded as traitors.

To appease the outrage felt in England, Eyre "The Butcher" was recalled, tried, and dismissed from the service. The Jamaican House of Assembly, unable to deal with the crisis, surrendered its power to the Crown, and Jamaica became a Crown Colony. Eventually, however, the colonists started agitating for the return of self-government.

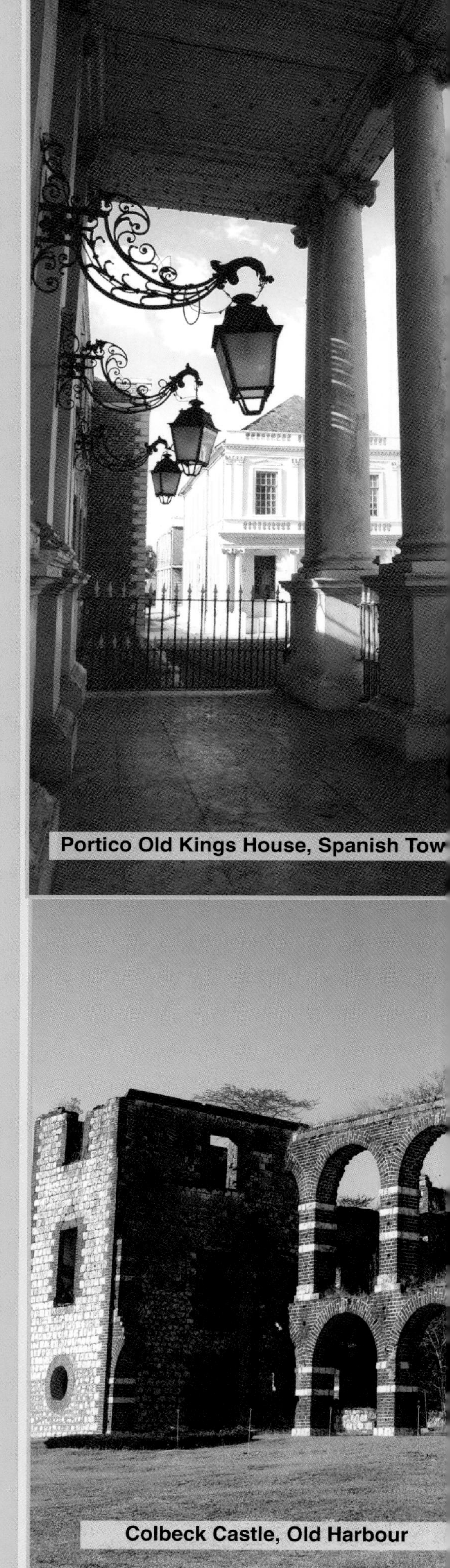

Portico Old Kings House, Spanish Tow

Colbeck Castle, Old Harbour

Emancipation Square, Spanish Town

Tharp House, Falmouth

View from Greenwood Great House, St. James

Parish Council Building, Spanish Town

Birth of a Nation

By 1938, Jamaica was ripe for the worst riots in its history. This time it was the longshoremen and sugar workers. Out of a small side-street office in Kingston emerged tall, lion-hearted, William Alexander Bustamante. While he organized a militant union, demanding higher wages and better social conditions, his cousin, Norman Washington Manley, barrister-at-law and former Rhodes Scholar, founded the Peoples National Party (PNP) and renewed the pressure for self-government.

Grudgingly, the British Parliament yeilded. In 1944, it granted a new constitution based on universal adult suffrage.

By 1953, the majority of power was finally transferred from 'The Man at King's House (the Governor), to an all-Jamaican elected parliament headed by a cabinet of ministers.

By 1959 colonialism had become internationally unpopular, and Britain's empire (pre-World War II) on which 'the sun never sets', had become a financial burden too grievous to be borne by the British.

Jamaica was one of the earliest colonies to be liberated. The process was peaceful; the final act – the Declaration of Independence – dramatic and sad for both. Jamaica and Britain have remained helpful friends.

With a penultimate amendment to the Constitution in 1959, the organized structure of Jamaica's government was delineated. The title 'Chief Minister' was upgraded to 'Premier', the British monarchial system retained, and Jamaicans started preparing for full independence. This was declared on August 6, 1962, replacing August 1 which had been allowed as Emancipation Day since 1838. In 2000 Emancipation Day as a holiday was reinstated.

Edna Manley Monument, Heroes Circle

Of the legion of Englishmen who governed Jamaica since 1655, the last three are the most vividly remembered. They are Sir Arthur Richards (Lord Milverton), the wartime 'tough guy' who played no favourites (he interned Bustamante and several others, inculding an Englishman, for the duration of World War II); Sir Hugh M. Foot (Lord Caenarvon), former British Ambassador to the U.N. and the diplomat who guided Jamaica through its constitutional teething period; and the very last of them, Sir Kenneth Blackburne, who became the first Governor General after Independence.

Island In The Sun

(Written by Irving Burgie)

Popularized by Harry Belafonte

This is my island in the sun,
Where my people have toiled since time begun,
I may sail on many a sea,
Her shores will always be home to me.

Chorus:
Oh, island in the sun,
Willed to me by my father's hand
All my days I will sing in praise,
Of your forest, waters, your shining sand.

When morning breaks the heav'n on high,
I lift my heavy load to the sky,
Sun comes down with a burning glow,
That mingles my sweat with the earth below.

Chorus:
I see woman on bended knee,
Cutting cane for her family,
I see man at the waterside,
Casting net at the surging tide.

Chorus:
I hope the day will never come,
That I can't awake to the sound of drums;
Never let me miss carnival
With ca-lyp-so song phil-o-soph-i-cal.

Chorus

The National Flag

"The sun shineth, the land is green and the people are strong and creative." This is the symbolism of the Jamaican National Flag. Black represents strength and creativity; Gold, natural wealth and beauty of sunlight; Green, hope and agricultural resources.

The National Pledge

Before God and all mankind, I pledge the love and loyalty of my heart, the wisdom and courage of my mind, the strength and vigour of my body in the service of my fellow citizens. I promise to stand up for Justice, Brotherhood and Peace, to work diligently and creatively, to think generously and honestly, so that Jamaica may, under God, increase in beauty, fellowship and prosperity, and play her part in advancing the welfare of the whole human race.

The National Anthem

Eternal Father, bless our land,
Guard us with Thy Mighty Hand,
Keep us free from evil powers,
Be our light through countless hours.
To our leaders, Great Defender,
Grant true wisdom from above.
Justice, truth be ours forever.
Jamaica, land we love.
Jamaica, Jamaica, Jamaica, land we love.

Teach us true respect for all,
Stir response to duty's call
Strengthen us the weak to cherish,
Give us vision lest we perish.
Knowledge send us Heavenly Father,
Grant true wisdom from above.
Justice, truth be ours forever,
Jamaica, land we love.
Jamaica, Jamaica, Jamaica, land we love.

The Streamer Tailed Humming Bird

(Doctor Bird) Trochilus Polytmus

(Second smallest bird in the world)

Blue Mahoe

Hibiscus elatus

Coat of Arms

The original Coat of Arms was designed by William Sandcroft, a former Archbishop of Canterbury. The original Latin motto, Indus Uterque Serveit Uni, was changed and Jamaicanized to Out of Many One People. An Awarak Indian man and woman stand on each side of a shield bearing a red cross with five golden pineapples superimposed on it. The crest is the Jamaican crocodile surmounting the Royal Helmet and Mantlings.

Ackee Fruit

Blighia sapida (The main ingredient of Jamaica's national dish, Ackee and Saltfish.)

Lignum Vitae Flower

Guiacum officinale

NATIONAL HEROES

In its search for national identity, Jamaica is discovering and enshrining its heroes. In the process, it is rewriting the British historical record, which chronicled some great native sons as "traitors". The government has reserved the title Right Excellent for those exalted to the status of National Hero.

Of the six heroes and one heroine, three emerge paramount. First and foremost is Marcus Mosiah Garvey (1887 – 1940), controversial 'father of the modern Negro', whose remains were brought from England and re-interred in National Heores' Park with pomp and ceremony.

For blacks the world over, whatever their language or politics, Marcus Garvey is a great hero. His doctrine of Garveyism, proclaimed through the Universal Nergo Improvement Association, which he founded in the USA, spiritually lifted the black man. It imbued his will and stroked his courage to declare his manhood and equality. It enabled him to assume the human dignity stripped from him through centuries of slavery, and to march forward into freedom and the sovereign independence we now enjoy throughout Africa and the West Indies. Garvey's life-sized statue stands in the centre of St. Ann's Bay, his birthplace.

Next are Sir William Alexander Bustamante (1884 – 1977), and Norman Washington Manley (1893 – 1969), contemporaries in the new Jamaica that began to take shape in 1938.

Bustamante, the colourful, courageous and resourceful labour leader and pragmatic politician who founded the Bustamante Industrial Trade Union (BITU) and the Jamaica Labour Party, died in August 1977 and was given the greatest state funeral Jamaicans have witnessed. He was buried at the National Shrine.

Norman Washington Manley

Marcus Mosiah Garvey

William Alexander Bustamante

Paul Bogle

George William Gordon

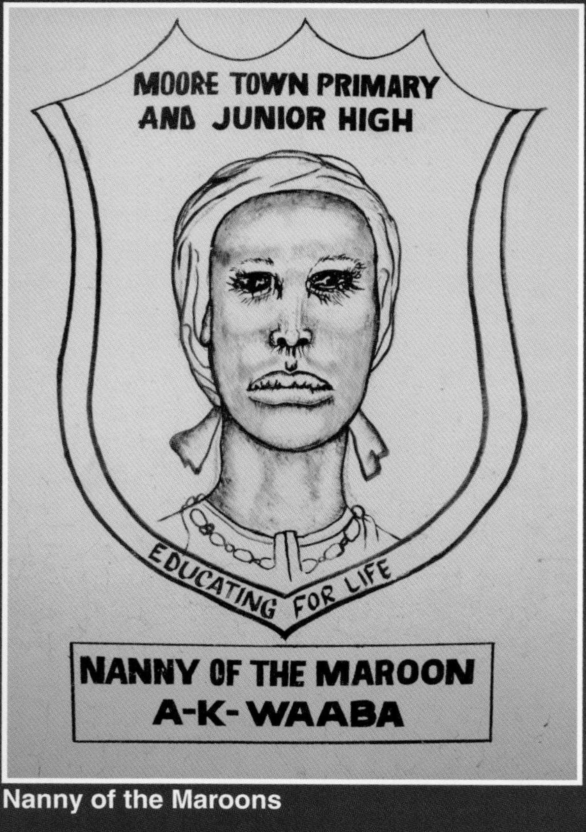

Nanny of the Maroons

Manley was a brilliant barrister who co-authored the Jamaican Constitution and founded the People's National Party, and deserves to be regarded by some as "Father of the Nation". His remains also lie in the National Shrine.

Each contributed greatly to the birth of modern Jamaica, and were responsible for wrestling it from the shackles of its colonial past.

Bustamante had the unique privilege of witnessing the unveiling of a bronze statue to his memory, which now stand at South Parade in the heart of Kingston, on the very pedestal where Queen Victoria's statue once stood. The latter is now located at St. William Grant Park. Manley's statue also stands in bronze at the Parade's northern entrance.

A fourth national hero is the tragic George William Gordon (1829 – 1865), whom the British also chronicled and hanged as a traitor in connection with the Morant Bay rebellion. This was his ironic reward for years of eloquent advocacy for more humane treatment of blacks.

His monument is Gordon House, the parliament building in Kingston which Norman Manley built when he was Premier.

The National Shrine is the centrepiece of National Heroes Park (formerly George VI Memorial Park), once a sand strewn race-course of 79 1/2 acres on the Kingston/St. Andrew border. The park also contains the War Memorial which was erected in1922. It honours those who died in both world wars.

The indomitable Paul Bogle (1820-1865) was a Baptist deacon who orchestrated the Morant Bay rebellion by leading a march from Stony Gut to Spanish Town in October 1865 with a group of over three hundred men and women who were disgruntled with the white planter class because of the injustice and unfairness that was meted out to them. The whites were uncompromising and refused to hear the cries of the blacks. A clash ensued in Morant Bay and when the dust had settled, the Custos, seventeen other officials, soldiers and seven of Bogle's men were dead. Troops were sent out the next day and a vicious fight took place between Bogle's men and the militia. Bogle was hanged and over four hundred and thirty men were killed.

The Morant Bay rebellion started out as a small riot but led to changes such as the Jamaican Assembly renouncing its charter and Jamaica becoming a Crown Colony. Governor Eyre was also recalled to England and the plight of the blacks social conditions were high-lighted. The new Governor was charged to take care of the interests of not only the white citizens but all citizens.

As the search into the past continues , a new hero and heroine have been recognized and enshrined. First is Nanny, the legendary female Maroon leader who, it is claimed, was able to catch live bullets with her bare hands. Second is Sam Sharpe, a former house slave who masterminded a bloody revolt in St. James parish, for which he was hanged. St. James Square in central Montego Bay has been renamed Sam Sharpe Square in his memory.

Other known heroes include Cudjoe (also spelled Kojo), Maroon chieftain, with whom the British signed a peace treaty after losing innumerable battles to his guerilla tactics; also Tacky, freedom fighter and folk hero who led an uprising known as "Tacky's War" in the parish of St. Mary in 1760.

Sam Sharpe

GOVERNANCE

Jamaica is a parlimentary democracy patterned after Britian. Its constitution guarantees legal equality to every citizen regardless of race, religion or color, as well as freedom of speech, assembly and government.

From1494 until 1655 the island belonged to Spain. In the 307 years following, it belonged to England, and was part of the British Empire, which no longer exists but has been partly replaced by the British Commonwealth of Nations.

Jamaica gained independence on August 6, 1962 and accepted the Queen of England as head of state. Her proxy is a Jamaican Governor General whom she appoints on the recommendation of the Prime Minister.

A debate is now taking place on constitutional reform but opinion is divided on the kind of constitution the country should have. Opinions range from maintaining the present Westminster form of government with its Constitutional Monarchy to a republican form of government with a ceremonial president to a full executive presidency similar to what exists in the United States.

The Jamaican Parliament consists of two Houses, the Senate and the House of Representatives. The Queen is titular head of Parliament, represented by the Governor General whose role is strictly formal. Once a year, at the official opening of Parliament, he delivers the "Throne Speech." Beyond this, his parliamentary function is limited to his formal assent to Bills passed by the two Houses.

The Senate (or "Upper House") is a nominated House made up of 21 Senators. Thirteen Senators are appointed by the Governor General on the advice of the

Top & Bottom: Jamaica House

Supporters of the People's National Party (PNP) at a political rally.

Prime Minister. The other eight are appointed on the advice of the Leader of the Opposition.

The House of Representatives (or "Lower House") consists of 63 members (the maximum allowed by the Constitution) elected under universal adult suffrage. Eighteen years is the legal voting age. Members are elected by single-member constituencies on a first-past-the-post basis.

The maximum life of a Parliament is five years, at the end of which it must be dissolved and a general electon held. However, the Prime Minister may advise the Governor General to dissolve Parliament any time within that period, and name a date for a general election. Parliament must also be dissolved and a general election held if a majority of all the members of the House of Representatives support a no-confidence motion against the Government.

The two parties which have alternated in leading Jamaica's government are: The People's National Party (PNP), founded by the late Rt. Excellent Norman Washington Manley, and the Jamaica Labour Party (JLP), founded by the late Rt. Excellent Sir William Alexander Bustamante, both of whom were instrumental in framing the Constitution.

Leader of the PNP is the Most Hon. Portia Lucretia Simpson-Miller.

Leader of the JLP is the Hon. Andrew Holness. He is the youngest person to have served as Prime Minister.

While there has been several attempts in the past to form other parties, none have taken firm hold. However, splits in the JLP and a growing discontent with the political process have spawned the National Democratic Movement which contested the election of

Supporters of the Jamaica Labour Party (JLP) at a political meeting.

1997, 2002 and in 2011 they won 265 votes, but no seat in Parliament.

The Prime Minister is selected by the majority party and is the island's chief administrator. The Cabinet is the policy making instrument appointed by the Prime Minister, who also has power to fire them. Each Ministry has a junior minister (or Minister of State) but the pivotal personality who helps to ensure order through changing administrations is a senior civil servant or permanent secretary.

Under a system of local government, the 13 parishes which comprises Jamaica (Kingston & St. Andrew being administratively one parish), have some measure of autonomy once their budgets have been approved by the central government. Each parish council is headed by a chairman, selected from among the elected councilors, and he also serves as Mayor in the parishes where this post exists. Councils are served by secretary/managers.

The government's administrative arm, excluding local government, is the Civil Service. Ministries are responsible for their departments, but can neither hire nor fire civil servants. This responsibilty rests with the Ministry of the Public Service.

Through numerous embassies and consulates, Jamaica maintains diplomatic relations with other countries. It has a non-aligned stance in world affairs, maintaining good relations with both East and West.

Vale Royal, Kingston. The official residence of the Prime Minister.

George William Gordon House

Left to right: The Hon. Syringa Marshall-Burnett, former President of the Senate and the Hon. Violet Nielson, former Speaker of the House of Representatives.

Parliament in session

PARADE OF PRIME MINISTERS

Since Independence in 1962, Jamaica has had nine Prime Ministers; six from the Jamaica Labour Party (JLP) and three from the People's National Party (PNP). Together they form Jamaica's two-party system of parliamentary government.

Prime Ministers, in order of succession, have been; Sir William Alexander Bustamante, who successively served for one and half terms and retired from parliament at age 80; Hugh Shearer, who finished Donald Sangster's term; Edward Seaga, who served two consecutive terms; and Michael Manley, who served his third term from February 1989 to March 1992 when he retired from politics, having previously served from 1972-1980. P.J. Patterson was then appointed Prime Minister and went on to serve four consecutive terms, a first in Jamaica's political history. He was succeeded by Portia Simpson-Miller who lost the 2007 general election to the JLP's Orette Bruce Golding. He served close to four years before stepping down and was succeeded by Andrew Holness, who is Jamaica's youngest Prime Minister to have served. He assumed office in October 2011 and lost in a land slide to the PNP two months later. Portia Simpson-Miller as leader of the PNP, became the Prime Minister of Jamaica in December 2012.

The Rt. Excellent Norman Manley, father of Michael Manley, served as Jamaica's Chief Minister and Premier immediately prior to Independence; Bustamante, Sangster, Shearer, Seaga, Golding and Holness belong to the JLP, and the Manleys, Patterson and Simpson-Miller to the PNP.

Under the constitution, each parliamentary term is for five years, but a Prime Minister may call an election at any time before the term ends, if he feels the political climate is favourable (Seaga in 1983), or if the government no longer reflects the people's wishes (Norman Manley in 1962; Michael Manley in 1980 and P.J. Patterson in 1993).

Bustamante retired from office due to illness, and Norman Manley retired while leading the parliamentary opposition. Both died in retirement and have been declared National Heroes. Their remains lie in National Heroes Park. Sangster, although not a National Hero, was certainly an eminent native son and he is also buried there; in an area set aside for Prime Ministers.

Shearer retired from politics in 1993 but was still President General of the Bustamante Industrial Trade Union (founded by Bustamante). He died at his home on July 5, 2004. Seaga was an elected Member of Parliament and leader of the opposition when he retired from politics in 2005. He is currently the Chancellor of the University of Technology.

Norman Washington Manley

The Rt. Excellent Norman Washington Manley M.M. Q.C., LL.B., National Hero (1883 – 1969), is widely acknowledged to be one of the most brilliant of Jamaican barristers of his time. The demand for freedom from colonial rule was already being made in 1938, the very peak of his legal career, when he co-founded the People's National Party (PNP) and became its president and began spearheading a determined, unapologetic campaign for independence.

Co-author of the Jamaican Constitution, he is fondly referred to as the " Father of the Nation"; being the author of changes which resulted first in representative government (1945) and later independence (1962). As Chief Minister (1955 – 1959), his main accents were on agriculture, education, industrial development, honest government and regional co-operation.

Sir William Alexander Bustamante

In his second consecutive term, the position having change from Chief Minister to Premier in 1959, he backed the doomed West Indies Federation and, three months later, he called a snap election, feeling duty-bound to seek a new mandate from the electorate. He lost the election and began once more to chafe in opposition.

He died in 1969, age 76, his memoirs unfinished. He did not live to see his statue raised at the northern entrance of the Parade in downtown Kingston, or to hear himself proclaimed a great Caribbean statesman and Jamaican National Hero.

The Rt. Excellent Sir William Alexander Bustamante, Kt. PC., G.B.E., LL.D., and National Hero (1884 – 1977), was Jamaica's first Prime Minister. Born William Alexander Clarke in Blenheim, Hanover, he later changed his name to Bustamante. A tower-tall spectacular personality of tremendous magnetism and force, as well as a spell-binding marathon orator; he emerged dramatically in May 1938 to lead the sugar, banana and shipping workers' revolt against "starvation wages".

Out of the revolt he fashioned the Bustamante Industrial Trade Union (BITU), and out of the BITU , the Jamaica Labour Party. He was fearless in his leadership and in his challenges to the bastions of colonialism.

Pragmatist and political counter-puncher, he laid no claims to statesmanship. "A little more bread and a little more butter", was the theme of his leadership campaign in 1944. Not infrequently did he drink whiskey all night with an employer and call strike on him the next day. Yet even capitalists loved him because, at heart, he understood them, having himself forsaken a profitable usury business to lead the workers' revolt.

At the age of 80 (two years after his second term as Prime Minister) he temporarily retired from parliament. Finance Minister Donald B. Sangster, his law-trained nephew and long time Man Friday, assumed the position of Acting Prime Minister. This temporary leave of absence was to become permanent.

On August 6, 1977, Bustamante died at the age of 93 and was buried with national and international honours.

The Most Honourable Sir Donald Burns Sangster, O.N., K.C.V.O., LL.B., was a spare-bodied, conservative, country lawyer and close confidante of Bustamante. Sangster served his party and his leader with loyalty and dedication, and with a solid, sound understanding of financial administration. It was only logical that he be chosen to serve out the remaining three years of Bustamante's second term. During those years, he closely followed the inherited policies and programs of Bustamante.

He led the JLP to victory in 1967 but only a month after becoming Prime Minister in his own right, he died, leaving history to ponder whether he would have changed his image from that of a "doer" to one of an innovator.

The Most Honourable Hugh Lawson Shearer, O.N., P.C., M.P., was the BITU's island supervisor. He assumed the role of Prime Minister upon the death of Donald Sangster. Shearer had long been the protégé of Bustamante, and was commonly known as the 'adopted son'.

A tall, handsome, irrepressible "bon vivant", he showed an impressive flair for foreign affairs during his term while sharing much of the burden of government with his Finance Minister, Edward Seaga.

Jamaica prospered economically under his term but due to neglect of some vital social developments and inter-party rivalry, the country voted Shearer and the JLP out of office on a platform of change. Shearer again teamed with Edward Seaga, this time as Deputy Prime Minister and Minister of Foreign Affairs, in the JLP-led government of 1980 – 1989. He retained his Clarendon seat in all elections until 1993.

Sir Donald Burns Sangster

Hugh Lawson Shearer

Edward Phillip George Seaga

The Most Honourable Edward Phillip George Seaga, O.N., P.C., M.P., B.A., was Jamaica's fifth Prime Minister. Medium-built, mild-mannered, eloquent and possessed of remarkable emotional control, he was seen as "the right man at the right time" in Jamaica's history. He took office in 1980 with an election campaign slogan of "Deliverance".

With unflappable calm and the encouraging and welcome assistance of friendly governments in both hemispheres, he set himself the task of guiding the now bankrupt country on to a path of economic recovery in which he was successful, achieving his target of 5% growth in 1988. He served a second consecutive term of office, and his overall tenure (1980 – 1989), was marked by structural readjustments, which sought to achieve economic growth by placing emphasis on the promotion of private enterprise, tourism and production for export.

Edward Seaga is Jamaica's longest serving Member of Parliament, having won his Western Kingston seat in 1962 and retained it until he retired from politics in 2005.

Michael Norman Manley

The Most Honourable Michael Norman Manley, O.N., P.C.,B.Sc., tall, handsome and charismatic, set in the mould of Bustamante and the second son of Norman Manley, was head of the NWU when he first assumed leadership of the country in 1972.

His first two terms in office were characterized by social programmes and alliances with other third-world countries and socialist governments. Democratic Socialism was declared as the ruling party's new political philosophy for Jamaica in 1974, heralding a period of increased ideological polarization within the country.

Although many of his social programmes were long overdue, his continuing shift to the left frightened many Jamaicans and overseas investors, leading to a flight of capital and people. The resulting economic decline was mainly responsible for his party's defeat in the 1980 general elections.

Manley was returned to office in February 1989, having convinced the electorate that his government would be politically moderate, and would "put people first". He retired from politics in 1992 due to illness and died in 1997.

The Most Honourable Percival James (P.J.) Patterson, O.N., P.C., Q.C, M.P., B.A., LLB., took over the prime ministership of the country on Manley's retirement from politics in 1992. Patterson's quiet but firm style of leadership is considered to be different from that of his predecessor. Under his leadership the PNP administration pursued a deepening of the liberalization of the economy and intensification of structrual adjustment. His regime led to the end of Jamaica's borrowing program from the International Monetary Fund (IMF). He led his party (PNP) to an unprecedented fourth term in office. He retired from politics in 2007.

Percival James Patterson

The Most Honourable Orette Bruce Golding, O.N., M.P., BSc, is Jamaica's eighth Prime Minister. He entered politics at an early age because of his father, Tacius Golding who was a Member of Parliament. At the tender age of 24, Bruce Golding became the youngest person to be elected to Jamaica's House of Representatives.

He was the founder of the National Democratic Movement after his split with the Jamaica Labour Party in 1995; he subsequently rejoined the JLP in 2002. His appointment as Prime Minister of the country was by a slim majority win in the 2007 elections against his PNP opponent Portia Simpson-Miller. His victory was nonetheless heralded as a significant blow to the opposition party that had been in power for 18 years.

Orette Bruce Golding

During his prime ministership he claimed the title of 'Chief Servant' of the people. His vision of Jamaica was

Andrew Michael Holness

to make it a place where 'everyone might not be rich, but no one has to be poor". With this vision in mind, the Prime Minister immediately abolished tuition fees in all public secondary schools within a year of his appointment and he also passed legislation that removed user fees at all public health facilities.

The Golding led administration in its short term sought to reshape the Jamaican political and social landscape, encourage investment and the development of infra-structure of the country so as to enable growth in the economy.

The Honourable Andrew Michael Holness, M.P., MSc. BSc, is Jamaica's ninth Prime Minister and the youngest in its history. He is a graduate of the University of the West Indies where he pursued a Bachelor of Science degree in management studies and a Master of Science degree in development studies. Holness was a protégé of Edward Seaga, a former Prime Minister of Jamaica. Holness became a Member of Parliament for West Central St. Andrew and served as opposition spokesperson on Land and Development from 1999 to 2002. In 2002, his portfolio was changed to Housing and again in 2005 to Education.

The year 2007 brought more changes to Holness' political career. With the Jamaica Labour Party elected to govern the country, he became the Minister of Education. Under his purview, the Jamaican education system saw considerable changes. There was a rise in literacy rates and the national education trust was founded to develop schools and to build new ones to alleviate the problems of overcrowding in the nation's high schools.

Andrew Michael Holness at the age of 39 was unanimously nominated by his party after Bruce Golding resigned as Prime Minister. Holness was sworn into office on October 23, 2011, however, his tenure was short-lived when he called the general elections on December 29, 2011. He lost the elections to the People's National Party.

The Most Honourable Portia Lucretia Simpson-Miller, O.N., M.P., B.A., became the first female Prime Minister of Jamaica when she took office in 2006. She has had an active life in politics spanning from 1974 when she won the Trench Town West division in Kingston and St. Andrew elections, for the People's National Party. She has held numerous positions such as Minister of Labour, Social Security and Sports where she brought improvements to the 'Overseas Farm Work Programme' and established the Overseas Recruitment Centre for Farm Work. She was also the Minister of Sports when Jamaica made its historic journey to the 1998 World Cup Football. Energetic, fiery and outspoken, 'Sister P' as she is affectionately called, has been a champion and a voice for the poor, dispossessed and voiceless. She is respected as an advocate for women and social justice. Simpson-Miller lost the general elections in 2007 to Bruce Golding but was re-elected as Prime Minister in December 2011 after the JLP lost the general election.

She is expected to chart the course of meeting the the social and economic needs of the country as it embarks on the journey of the next fifty years.

Portia Lucretia Simpson-Miller

Left: Prime Minister Simpson-Miller as she appeared in *Time* Magazine's *100 Most Influential People in the World*.

HEADS OF STATE

His Excellency. The Most Honourable Sir Patrick Linton Allen, O.N., GCMG, C.D., was installed as the sixth person and the fifth native Governor General on February 26, 2009. A devout Christian, he has served the Seventh Day Adventist church in a number of positions for 28 years. He has served as a Pastor, Principal, Director and President in the Central Jamaica Conferences and the West Indian Union Conference respectively.

As a member of the Commonwealth, Jamaica's Executive Authority remains vested in Her Majesty, Queen Elizabeth II. However, Jamaica's Constitution provides for her to be represented by a Governor General whom she appoints, on recommendation of the Prime Minister.

The role of Govenor General is primarily a ceremonial one as real legislative and executive power is in the hands of the elected representatives of the people. Among his ceremonial duties are administering the oath of office to the parliamentarians, judges and public servants of senior rank and appointing to life-long service the Custodes for the fourteen parishes.

These Custodes perform ceremonial roles on behalf of the Governor General and are the responsible body for the confirmation of the appointments of Justices of the Peace.

Without his presence, no public ceremonial occasion is complete; he presents honours and exercises the prerogative of mercy on behalf of the Queen; under the Constitution, he is given authority to act in many matters, but almost always on the advice of the government or the Privy Council.

SIR KENNETH BLACKBURN (1957-1962), *Jamaica's last English Governor who served as Governor General in the months before independence was declared.*

SIR CLIFFORD CAMPBELL (1962-1973), *Jamaica's first native Governor General.*

SIR FLORIZEL GLASSPOLE (1973-1991), *Jamaica's longest serving Governor General who retired from the post in 1991.*

SIR HOWARD COOKE (1991-2006), is *Jamaica's third native Governor General.*

The Privy Council consists of six members appointed by the Governor General after consultation with the Prime Minister. The function of the Privy Council is usually limited to advising the Governor General on the exercise of the royal prerogative of mercy and the discipline of the civil service, local government officers and the police, in cases where appeals are made. The Governor General's secretary also holds the position of Clerk of the Privy Council. Two extremely demanding and busy posts where the real work is done.

Despite his limited powers, the schedule of the Governor General is a heavy one. Without his assent, no bill passed in Parliament can become law. As an imperative formality, all incoming foreign diplomats present their credentials to him. Every visitor on the slightest pretext may visit King's House, his official residence. He is also patron of many causes and organizations whose functions are incomplete without the eminence of his presence.

Should the Governor General be unable to perform his duties temporarily, for whatever reason, he may, on the advice of the Prime Minister, appoint any person in Jamaica to be his deputy. This is usually the longest serving Custos.

Like the Queen of England, his role and title carry no real independent authority but his presence represents the crucial link betwwen Jamaica and the Commonwealth of Nations.

SIR KENNETH HALL (2006-2009), *he became Jamaica's Governor General in February 2006.*

SIR PATRICK ALLEN (2009-present), *Jamaica's sixth Governor General and the fifth Jamaican to hold this position since independence in 1962.*

Top & Bottom: Kings House

A policeman on patrol

Police officers at an event at the National Stadium

LAW & ORDER

Jamaica has gone through some turbulent times in its recent history, but no more so than any country in today's world with a large population crowded on small land space and with high unemployment. Kingston, the capital and most densely populated part of the island, has experienced most of the problems in its inner city areas. In the resort areas, the only crime worth worrying about is the trafficking of ganja and hard drugs.

In the seventies, the old Ministry of Home Affairs and Justice was replaced by the Ministry of National Security and Justice. Parliament passed new, tougher legislation to give law enforcement swifter, heavier and surer clout, with tighter control on firearms.

Law, order and justice in Jamaica begins with the cop on the beat. By any standards, Jamaica is a fairly well policed state – though a far cry from a police state. The Jamaica Constabulary Force is stepping up recruiting measures, including women, and a volunteer force of civilians, through 'Neighbourhood Watches", under the jurisdiction of the police, is recruited to augment district crime patrols.

Independence brought "Jamaicanization" and sophistication. This includes ground and air mobility, modern scientific criminology, links with Interpol, Scotland Yard, the FBI and other international law enforcement agencies. Jamaica also has extradition treaties with several countries. Close liasions between Jamaica's Criminal Investigation Department (CID) and the U.S. Narcotics Division have not eliminated the island as a major link in the northward flow of hard drugs, but the Jamaican police maintain a vigilance that keeps

Jamaica Constabulary Force

chalking up significant results in intercepted drug shipments and arrests.

In an effort to combat corruption, the government passed the Corruption Prevention Act in 2000, with the aim of appropriately punishing members of the public service, which includes the Jamaica Constabulary Force. To strengthen its resolve against corruption, the force also established an Anti-Corruption Branch (ACB), whose motto is "Integrity is non-negotiable". This replaced its Internal Affairs Division.

Crime Stop is a partnership between the community, the police and the media designed to involve the public in the fight against crime. Crime Stop encourages the public to give information by offering total anonymity to all callers and, for those who wish, a cash reward for information that leads to an arrest, recovery of stolen property or the seizure of illegal drugs or guns. The programme is administered by the National Crime Prevention Fund and is run under the direction of The Private Sector Organisation of Jamaica. It was officially launched on September 6, 1989 and has been a successful initiative. In 2011, investigations stemming from the calls to Crime Stop led to the seizure of narcotics valued at approximately $45.5 million and the recovery of property valued at approximately $17.2 million.

The Jamaica Defence Force (JDF), comprising a standing army of both men and women, derives from the old tough-fibred West India Regiment which covered itself with glory whilst fighting as a part of the British Imperial army in Egypt, Africa and Europe. The JDF worked alongside the

The Jamaican Military Band

Jamaica Coast Guard

Jamaica Constabulary Force against criminal and subversive elements within the island.

The JDF Chief of Defence Staff keeps his army in a state of combat readiness second to none in the British Caribbean. The army consists of four battalions, an air wing and the Coast Guard, all commanded from a unified headquarters based at Up Park Camp in Kingston. Other bases are in the parishes of St. Andrew, St. Ann, St. James, Manchester, St. Mary, and the old pirate city of Port Royal.

Jamaica is unlikely to ever declare war on any of her neighbours. If affected, she is guaranteed speedy help from Britain, Canada and the U.S.A. with whom she has mutual assistance pacts. Like the Police, the Army comes under the Ministry of National Security and Justice, and they both constitute the security forces.

Jamaica's legal and judicial system is based on English Common Law. The judicial function is to interpret, apply and enforce the laws of Jamaica in cases where the laws are infringed or alleged to be infringed, or where contention arises between different parties. The Judiciary is made up of: A Chief Justice and Puisne Judges in the Supreme Court and Court of Appeal, Resident Magistrates in R.M. Courts, Coroners Court, Traffic Court, Justices of the Peace in Petty Sessions, Tribunals or inquiries.

The lowest court is the Petty Sessions, once called "the Poor Man's Theatre", while the Resident Magistrates Courts provide the work loads of the various Circuit Courts (Parish Assizes).

Other arms of Justice, separate from the Judiciary establishment, are the Attorney

General, Director of Public Prosecutions, Crown Solicitor and Ombudsmen.

The Chief Justice is appointed by the Governor General on recommendation by the Prime Minister after consultation with the Opposition leader. Like all other judges, and under the present Constitution, he may only be removed from office by sanction of the Queen to whom he, and all senior public servants, swear allegiance.

The Privy Council of England still remains the final court of appeal in all criminal cases, except, perhaps, Petty Session cases. This would cease should Jamaica become a republic. The creation of the Caribbean Court of Justice also threatens the Privy Council being the final appellate court.

In 2005, the Privy Council ruled that the CCJ bill that was passed in Parliament in 2004 was unconstitutional. This bill would have made the CCJ the final appellate court in Jamaica. There continues to be a raging debate whether Jamaica should make it its final appellate court.

Jamaica Defence Force soldier

Instances of corrupt or politically biased judges are rare in Jamaica. The poor continue to depend on the "blindfolded lady with the unbalanced scales" but, by and large, the twin machinery of Law and Justice works with reasonable equity. The Security Forces, combining Police and Army, do a commendable job of law enforcement, fully supported by the government.

ARCHITECTURE

To satisfy his instinctive need of shelter from the elements and his enemies, man built his way out of caves progressively, through mud, grass, brick, wood and iron, developing architectural variety and stability, mastering new techniques in both design and construction.

Gradually experimenting with combinations of materials, he evolved new structural designs to meet different climatic conditions, and also to satisfy and express his growing consciousness that grace and beauty could be achieved together. Discovering the superior tensile strength of steel over iron, he added floor upon floor until, by the mid-19th century when concrete began to replace bricks, he emerged with the skyscraper that, in this century, has turned the streets of his principal cities into canyons with myriad eyes of gleaming glass.

As residential and resort land prices move skyward and the population continues to multiply, middle and upper-level income Jamaicans may find themselves living higher and higher above ground, in less and less square footage.

In commendable but often misguided efforts to house the masses, successive governments have perpetuated a wasteful policy of "spread-out" projects; meanwhile, far-sighted economists and sociologists pray the day will quickly dawn when government planners will discover that it is easier and less costly to reach for the sky, than to spread mass housing over land that is capable of growing crops or cattle.

For economy of energy, another opinion holds that future residential buildings might not go higher than three floors. Environmentalists hope that developers

St. Hilda's High School

Meeting room ceiling at the Conference Centre

Metcalfe Market, Annotto Bay

Ruins of the Old Morant Bay Courthouse

might give more consideration to conserving the vegetation, rather than eradicating whole acreages willy-nilly, in the interests of cost efficiency. The effects of wanton destruction of tropical rain forests – and our own forests here – are already being felt worldwide in the rising global temperatures.

Spanish Jamaica (1494 – 1655) was built with wood, stone and mortar, following mostly Moorish architectural patterns. British Jamaica (1655 – 1962) tended towards pragmatism, conscious of the need to keep out light and let in air for natural ventilation and cooling. Brick brought as ballast from England, and locally quarried stone, were favoured for foundations as well as whole structures. Cut stone and mortar were preferred for churches, many of which have stood intact through numerous earthquakes and hurricanes.

Top and bottom: Early 1900s architecture

Human abodes in the era of the English were of two extremes: the Great House of the rich mercantile class, planters and penkeepers, and the barracks and hovels of the blacks. But as a mulatto class came of age, skilled craftsmen among them filled the space between with the gingerbread house as evidence of a growing middle class sophistication.

These lovely buildings are disappearing fast, their sites taken by designs that combine almost every type of architecture known to modern man, and embodying materials of the age of synthetics.

The first flat roof, an Egyptian original copied by the Romans, came to Jamaica as late as the mid-1940s when an enterprising young developer named Sandy Watkins built a concrete block-and-steel prototype on a site in Meadowbrook, St. Andrew, to bait buyers to his middle-income project. Since then, many Jamaicans have opted for the flat roof design. All government mass housing also features the flat roof design.

Modern Jamaica is an architectural mix of the proceeding eras as well as imported styles adapted to suit the climate, the terrain, and to withstand the effects of natural disasters.

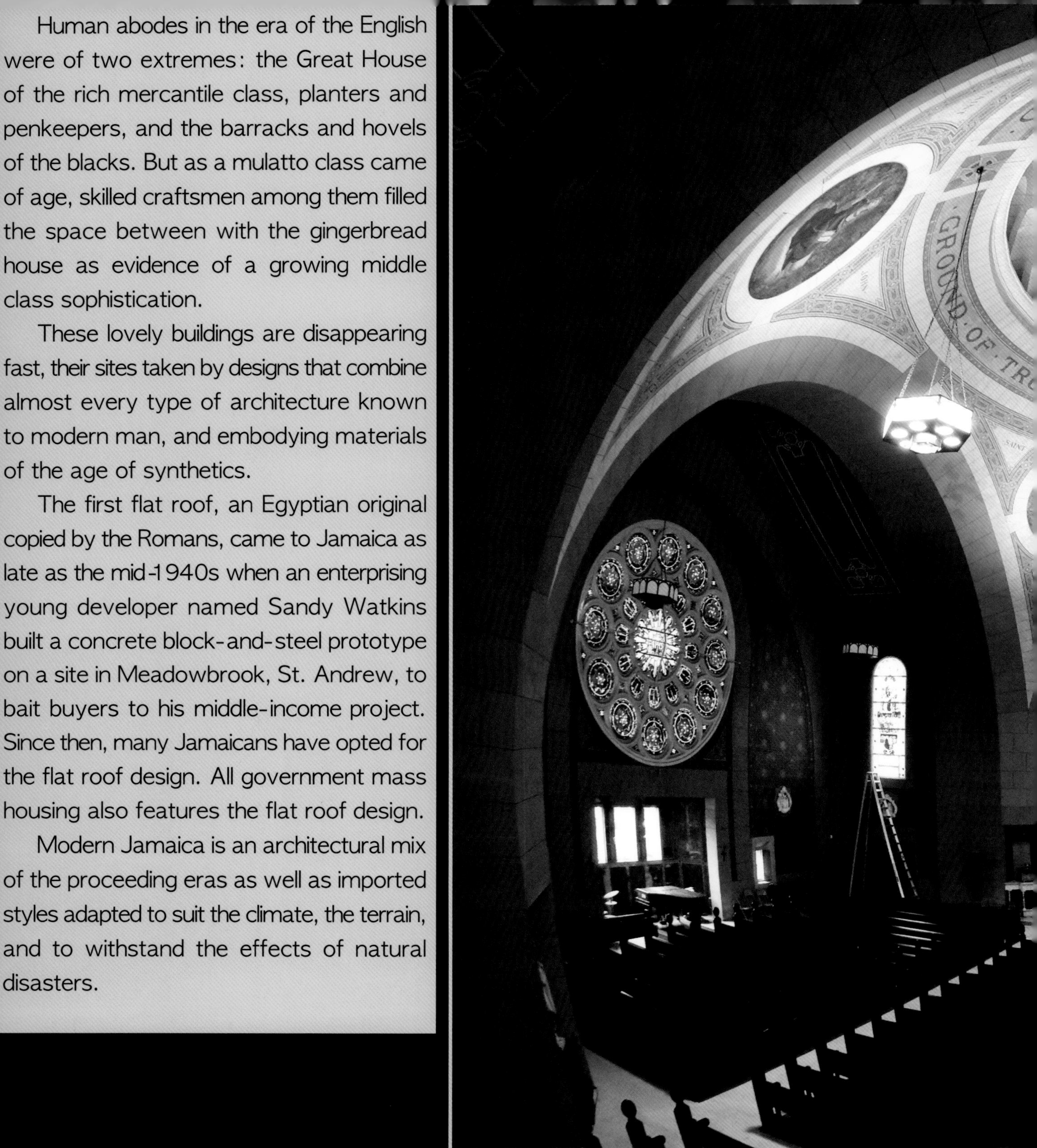

The interior of Holy Trinity Roman Catholic Cathedral, North Street, Kingston

Above are different views of the Half-Way-Tree Transport Centre

Mount Herman Baptist Church, Riversdale, St. Catherine

Stain glass inside Holy Trinity Roman Catholic Cathedral, North Street, Kingston

Devon House

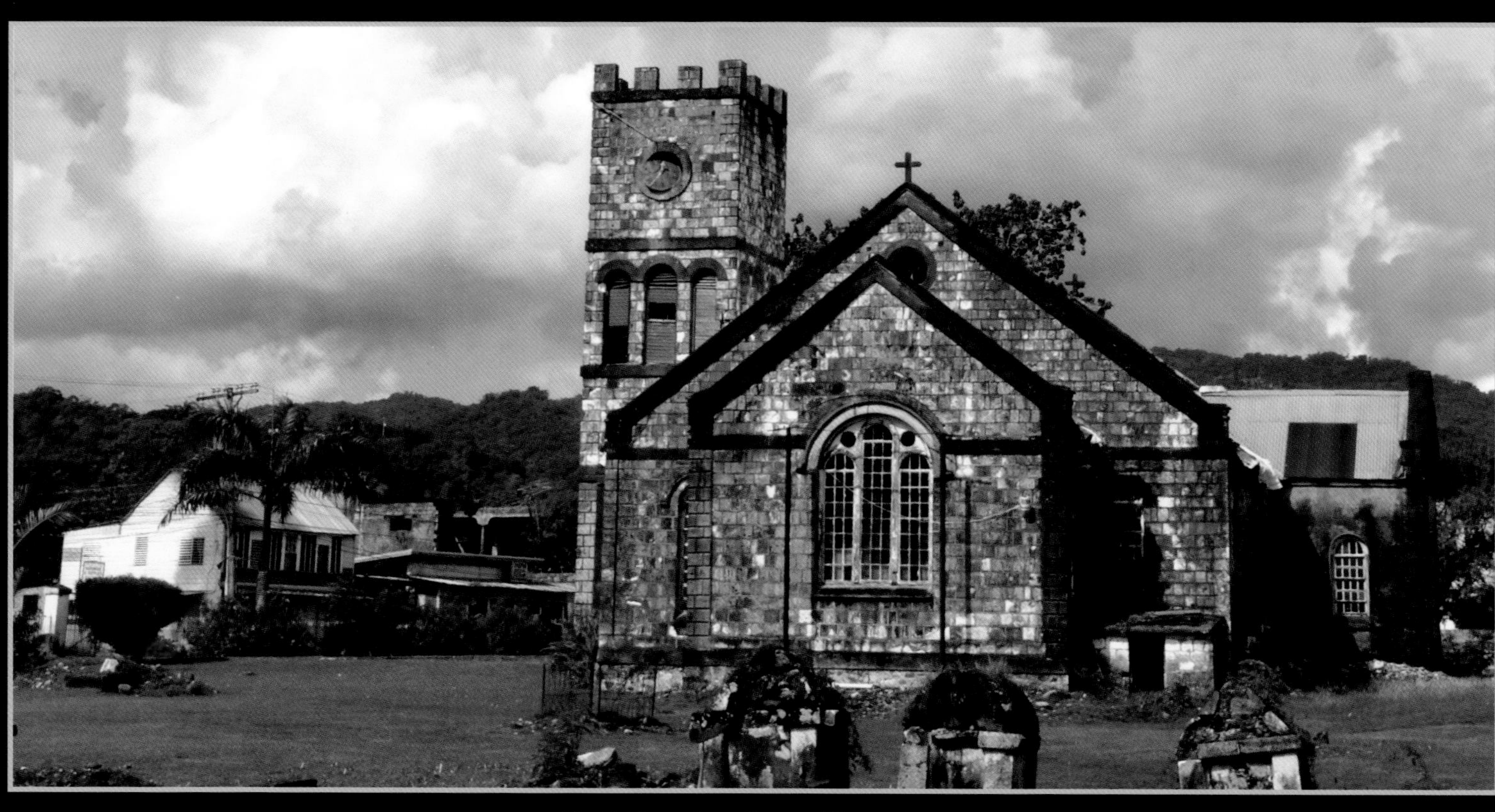

Buff Bay Anglican Church

Top: Lucea Court House
Bottom: Heritage House

HISTORICAL TOWNS

The Phoenix Foundry, Falmouth

Court House Clock, Lucea

Old Post Office, Falmouth

Trelawny Drive, Falmouth

FALMOUTH is a quaint town that is rich and vibrant with history. It is located 18 miles east of Montego Bay. It is noted for being one of the Caribbean's best-preserved Georgian towns. Founded in 1769 by Thomas Reid, Falmouth became the capital of Trelawny around 1790. It was named after Falmouth, Cornwall in England which was the birthplace of Sir William Trelawny, who was governor of Jamaica at the time.

The new capital experienced a 'boom' in its early years and it was not unusual to see nearly thirty ships at the Falmouth Harbour unloading cargo and taking on sugar, rum, etc. The ports generated considerable employment and sailors swarmed the town spending lavishly. The streets were lined with beautiful houses with unique fretwork and windows. Falmouth became the play ground for the rich and famous. It was one of the first towns in the western hemisphere to have piped water; even before New York City.

Falmouth experienced wealth until its gradual decline in the late nineteenth century. By the 1920s, the economic vibrancy that once existed in Falmouth had shifted to Kingston, the capital of Jamaica.

Falmouth is now experiencing a renewed vibrancy with the development of the town and a new port that was built to accommodate the Oasis of the Seas and other large cruise ships. The port was opened in early 2011 and welcomed numerous tourists. The town is on its way to its days of former glory.

Falmouth Town Square

Cast Iron Bridge, Spanish Town

The Rodney Memorial, Spanish Town

PLACES OF INTEREST IN FALMOUTH:

Falmouth courthouse: This was built in 1915. It's one of the first official buildings in the town. It was destroyed by fire and was rebuilt in 1926.

St. Peter's Anglican Church: Built in 1795, it is one of the oldest buildings in the town. It is constructed of brick and stone. It is a perfect example of the classic architectural form of the era. There are two galleries in the church and graves over two hundred years old can be found in the cemetery.

Falmouth All-age school: Currently housed on a former army barracks, Fort Balcarres.

Good Hope Great House: 18th century Great House that overlooks the Queen of Spain Valley, Martha Brae River and the Cockpit mountains.

SPANISH TOWN, once called Villa de la Vega is the capital of the parish of St. Catherine. It is built on the West Bank of the Rio Cobre and lies thirteen miles from Kingston on the main road. Once the capital of Jamaica from the 16th to the 19th Century, Spanish Town has had many other names over the centuries, such as Santiago de la Vega and St. Jago de la Vega, this is evidence of the two colonial periods that shaped its history. The two periods were the Spanish 1494-1655 and the English 1655-1962. Spanish Town is home to a number of memorials and the National Archives. It has one of the oldest Anglican Churches outside of England and is the oldest city to have been continuously occupied in the Western Hemisphere. The history of Spanish Town is evident and is preserved in the old buildings and the names of the streets.

SOME NOTABLE SITES:

Old Kings House: Notable because it was on the steps of Kings House that the proclamation of Emancipation was read on August 1, 1838. It was also the residence of the Governor until 1872 when Kingston became the capital of Jamaica. Only the front of the building still remains as the rest of it was destroyed by fire in 1925.

The Spanish Town Cathedral: It is the oldest Anglican Cathedral in the former British colonies.

The House of Assembly: This is where the parliamentarians met to discuss the political, social and economic direction of the colony. It was built in 1762.

The Rodney Memorial: This commemorates Admiral George Rodney who fought at the Battle of the Saints in 1782 against the combined fleet of the Spanish and French. The National Archives are next door to the memorial and is home to a number of interesting documents.

Old Iron Bridge: The Cast Iron Bridge was erected in 1801 at a cost of 4,000 pounds. It was designed by Thomas Wilson of England and manufactured by Walker and Company of Rotherham in England. The bridge spans 29.7 metres and stands as the oldest iron bridge of its kind in the western hemisphere.

SOME NOTABLE STREETS:

Monk Street: It was given its name because of the monastery that was once there.

Nugent Street: Named after British Colonial Governor George Nugent

Manchester Street: Its name was derived from William Montagu, who was the fifth Duke of Manchester. He was also a British Colonial Governor.

Spanish Town is home to most of Jamaica's early history. Balls, galas and fetes were held there. It was the entertainment hub. In popular culture, it should be noted that Bertha Antionettea Mason, the insane wife of Edward Rochester in Charlotte Bronte's accredited novel *Jane Eyre*, was from Spanish Town. Calico Jack and his crew were also hanged in Spanish Town in 1720. Asafa Powell, one of Jamaica's greatest sprinters is also from Spanish Town. Spanish Town is a historian's dream.

PORT ROYAL:

"Wine and women drained their wealth to such a degree that...some of them became reduced to beggary. They have been known to spend 2 or 3,000 pieces of eight in one night; and one gave a strumpet 500 to see her naked. They used to buy a pipe of wine, place it in the street, and oblige everyone that passed to drink" said Charles Leslie when he wrote the History of Jamaica. In its heyday Port Royal was debauchery central because of the excessive drinking of the pirates, prostitution and every moral deficiency known to man in the 16th and 17th Century. It had gained the reputation of the Sodom of the New World. It is said that Port Royal had one drinking house per every ten residents. The city was so wealthy that coins were created to be used as payment rather than the usual system of barter. It was a commercial Mecca with pirates plying the shipping lanes.

Founded in 1518, Port Royal is located at the end of the Palisadoes strip and was the capital of Jamaica before it was destroyed in the 1692 earthquake. The earthquake and subsequent tsunami killed nearly half of the population. Some believed it was punishment from God because of the sinful ways of the residents. Fort Charles survived, but Fort James, Carlisle and Rupert sank. The city was eventually rebuilt over the centuries but a devastating earthquake on January 14, 1907 destroyed most of what was built.

Today, Port Royal is known as the sunken city with some of the most fascinating archaeological relics in the western hemisphere.

HISTORICAL SITES:

Fort Charles: "You, who tread his footprints, remember his glory" reads the plaque that is in memory of Admiral Horatio Nelson who was once stationed here. The fort is well preserved and well worth seeing.

Giddy House: The former artillery store, it is so named because of how it is tilted; a result of the 1907 earthquake.

Port Royal Marine Laboratory of the University of the West Indies: It was founded in 1955. The laboratory is used to teach marine biology and marine ecology.

Fort Charles Maritime Museum: Located in the old British naval hospital, it exhibits man's relationship to the sea, from the time of the Tainos to the present.

Giddy House, Port Royal

Fort Charles, Port Royal

Port Royal Marina

SOME HERITAGE SITES ACROSS THE ISLAND

PORT ANTONIO

DeMontevin Lodge: It was built in 1881 and is an eclectic mix of the Victorian architectural style, with Gingerbread details. The building's decorative ironwork was designed and cast in Scotland.

Folly Point Lighthouse: Built in 1888, the tower is constructed of masonry and is fire proof.

LIONEL TOWN

Portland Point Lighthouse: It has the highest tower in the island, standing at a height of 145 feet.

St. Peter's Church: One of the oldest churches in Jamaica. It was founded in 1671 as the parish church of the former parish of Vere. The present building was erected around 1715 on the foundation of the original. The church bell weighs a quarter ton and was commissioned by the same company that created Big Ben, London's most distinguishing landmark.

MAY PEN

Halse Hall Great House: One of the island's historic houses, its history began during the Spanish occupation of Jamaica when the estate was named "Hato de Buena Vista" (Ranch of the beautiful view). When Jamaica fell to the British in 1655, the property was gifted to Thomas Halse, a British soldier.

LUCEA

Fort Charlotte: This was built in the mid 18th Century by the British for the defence of the North North Westerly coast.

SANTA CRUZ

Lover's Leap: Named after two legendary slave lovers from the 18th century who leaped to their deaths rather than face capture and separation, Lover's Leap consists of a cliff with a drop of approximately 1,700 feet.

KINGSTON

Papine-Mona Aqueduct: A fine example of civil engineering in 18th Century Jamaica, the Aqueduct onced served Mona, Hope and Papine Estates with water from the Hope River. It was built by Thomas Hope Elleston in 1758.

MONTEGO BAY

Rose Hall Great House: The greatest of Jamaican great houses, the Rose Hall Great House was built in 1770 by John Palmer and his wife. It eventually became the residence of their grandnephew, John Rose Palmer. In 1820, Palmer married Annie, a beautiful English girl who became known as the White Witch of Rose Hall.

OCHO RIOS

Rio Nuevo Battle Site: The site of the final pitched battle between British and Spanish forces to determine possession of Jamaica.

MOORE TOWN

Nanny Town: Possibly the most sacred of all Maroon sites and is named after the great Maroon leader, Nanny, who is Jamaica's only national heroine. It was from this strategically located stronghold in the parish of Portland, that Nanny launched her wars against the British Colonial Government.

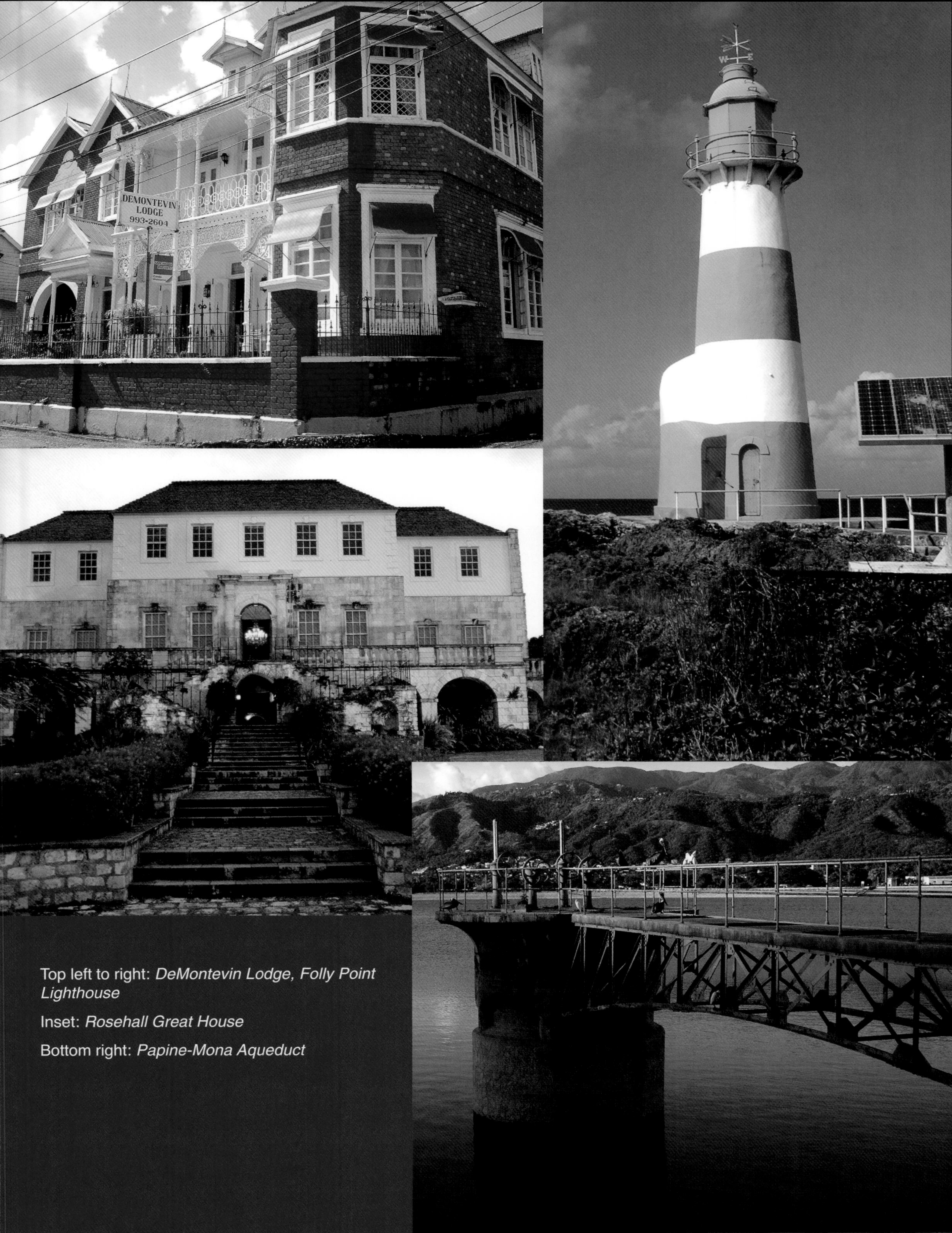

Top left to right: *DeMontevin Lodge, Folly Point Lighthouse*

Inset: *Rosehall Great House*

Bottom right: *Papine-Mona Aqueduct*

FACES OF JAMAICA

In the pre-dawn of Jamaican history, there were Tainos, a peaceful, carefree people. They lived in simple harmony with the fruitful land and the abundance of the surrounding sea, fearing only the deities which dwelt, they believed, in storms, in the sun, moon, lakes, rivers, mountains and clouds.

The Spaniards, led by Columbus, rudely interrupted this idyll in 1494. They came to exploit the New World, and their attitude was tough and ruthless. No one is certain how many Tainos were in Jamaica when Spain colonized the island, but whatever the number, they were unable to withstand the invading Spaniards. They were conquered and distributed to work as servants and labourers. The work was harsh and punishment cruel and in a short while, the Tainos were dying like flies.

To replace them, the Spaniards captured Fantis, Bushmen, Mandingos, Ibos, Coromantes and Ashantis from Africa, importing them to Jamaica when it was learnt that there was no significant amount of gold to be had. Vast rich areas were discovered in Mexico and settlers had stopped coming to Jamaica. But many remained, becoming ranchers and farmers, and a few went in for shipbuilding, tanning, cloth making and shop-keeping. In a short while, in the small neglected colony of Jamaica, a strange thing happened. An intimacy developed among all the remaining people: Spaniards, Africans and the few remaining Tainos, and mixtures of all three. When pirates raided, they got together and fought or fled to the hills if the enemy was too strong.

By the time the English invaded the island in 1655, one English writer was horrified to find a situation resulting in

near equality among all classes. One reason for the tolerant atmosphere may have been that the Spanish-Jamaicans came from parts of Spain where people of African descent had lived for a long time. Many were accustomed to black and brown faces, and they had not the same barrier of ethnic ingnorance to overcome, as would the British. Whatever the reason, racism, which was to assume such ugly proportions under the British, appeared to be almost absent from Spanish Jamaica.

On May 11, 1655, the Spanish surrendered to the British, but while the terms of surrender were being worked out, some of the Africans and Spanish-Jamaicans made off into the interior. There they fought beside each other for several years under the flag of Spain as they tried to drive out the British.

In the early days of the struggle for possession of Jamaica, it often seemed to the British that the most aggressive and dangerous element of the Spanish force were the Africans. They had all the qualities of good hunters. They were strong, enduring, skilled in the use of weapons, unaffected by inclement weather and rough terrain. They also had no reason to regard the British as anything but pirates and looters and thus the fighting continued.

Jamaica remained under martial law until 1663, when civilian government was established. The British also established a plantation system using indentured servants from their own country; downtrodden fellow Englishmen condemned into exile for crimes both real and fancied. Unable to withstand the hard labour of toiling in the fields in the blazing sun, as well as malaria and other

fevers, which plagued them, they soon had to be replaced with Africans.

By the 1670s many of these Africans were breaking out of the estates in search of freedom, joining forces with the remnants of the Spanish-Jamaicans and other Africans in the mountainous interior. This loose band of freedom fighters became Maroons, a word of uncertain derivation and meeting. In Jamaica it came to mean a fugitive or guerilla fighter, one whose spirit could not be broken by man.

All kinds of influences go into the making of a nation, the predominant ones usually characterizing the people of that nation. And so it was with Jamaica.

More settlers followed: from the bogs of starving Ireland, with their unquenchable laughter, haunting melodies, their love for brawling and liquor; from dreary Wales, where every coal mine was a cemetery for the poor man; from Germany on false promises of unlimited land; from famine-wrecked China with its rampaging warlords and pitiful starvation; from India

where flood and famine were Nature's way of life. These were the early settlers in Jamaica.

Under the tropical sun, white bred with black and brown, begetting hosts of mulatto children who would soon demand "white" rights. White bred with oriential as East met West in a heady, intoxicated embrace, recklessly, unconsciously, producing a unique new nation.

In the succeeding centuries of time, racial bloodlines have become blurred and family trees have produced multi-coloured fruit, which defy the tracings of the most eminent anthropologists. Black is indelible. Indeed, black is the pervading colour, making up nine-tenths of the nation. But no-one is ever sure that even the blackest face is without trace of some other racial strain, in this small island to which so many races came and have lived as one for so many centuries of recorded time.

They are a new race, a new breed, proud of their multiracialism. Proud too of their common heritage and language, of their culture of all the races from which they spring. They are proud, above all, of their national motto: "Out of Many, One People". Indeed and in fact, Jamaicans are one people.

'Out of Many, One People' typified in this photograph of school children.

RELIGION

Jamaican theologian, Dr. Horace Russell, defines religion as "that working belief by which all humans interpret themselves in relation to the world, and the nature of things and events beyond their own and immediate personal control, and by which they also interpret themselves".

Accepting this definition, Jamaicans interpret themselves through many religions, some dating back to slavery, and some comparative new comers to the local scene. Under the freedom enshrined in the Constitution, the Jamaican is free to serve any god in whatever way he chooses. He exercises this choice through denominations as varied as the skin-shades of the population of which he is a part.

Religion means a lot to the Jamaican, especially the rural dwelling ones. It consoles him for the wrongs and deprivations he endures in daily life; it curbs his urges to violence when provoked to anger. His obedience to man-made laws is rooted more in his respect for the Ten Commandments and Christ's teachings, than in his fear of mortal punishment.

His places of worship range from bamboo-framed, thatch-roofed shacks in the remote villages, to stained-glass cathedrals in the towns. East Indians, last of the indentured laborers, brought with them the Hindu and Muslim faiths. Jews have their beautiful synagogue in Kingston.

Oldest is the Roman Catholic religion, which came with Columbus in 1494. Then came the Jews, who emigrated to Jamaica when Portugal was joined to the Spanish crown in 1580. Following were the Anglicans (1655 – the year Penn and Venables arrived), the

Candles burning at a Revivalist wake

St. Peter's Anglican Church, Alley

Anglican Priests celebrating the Eucharist

A Rastafarian

St. Peter's Anglican Church, Port Royal

ST. ANDREW PARISH CHURCH

St. Andrew Parish Church, Half-Way-Tree

Moravians (1754), the Methodists (1789) , the Presbyterians (1824), and the Congregationalists (1876). These were all European religions. Baptists came from America with the Virginian ex-slave, George Lisle, in 1783, and with an infusion from England in 1814.

The records are unclear regarding the arrival of Islam, but evidence of its existence in the island goes back as far as 1840. East Indians brought Hinduism and the Muslim faith in the early 1800's when the Indians took the place of freed Negro slaves on the plantations.

By the beginning of the 20th century, the Jamaica mission field was being well served. Before the first quarter was over, the Disciples of Christ, the Society of Friends, the Salvation Army, Jehovah's Witnesses and Seventh Day Adventists were also reaping harvests of converts, whilst at the same time helping to broaden the base of education laid by the British colonial government.

By December 6 1992 the battle for Jamaican souls was so intense that Presbyterians and Congregationalists, two of the grass roots religions, wisely merged into the United Church of Jamaica and Grand Cayman, to more effectively hold their ground.

Some of the new religions that came after World War I collided head-on with old cults such as Pocomania, Mayalism and Revivalism, salvaged by former slaves from the religions they brought from Africa but were forbidden to practice under pain of death.

Like Voodooism in Haiti, each had a content of Chistianity. Despite the vigour of some of the newer imports, Rastafarianism- founded in the early 30s by one L.P. Howell, on an abandoned plantation called Pinnacle in St. Catherine – has confounded the nation with its growth.

University of the West Indies, Mona Chapel

A baptism at a local river

Kingston Parish Church

Haile Selassie, late emperor of Ethiopia, was born as Ras (Prince) Tafari Makonen in Harare. Rastafarianism is nothing more or less than the Africanization of the white God symbol for a black one – Haile Selassie, to whom is ascribed distant kinship with King Solomon. Rastafarianism has, however, run up against the law by the ritualistic and widespread use of ganja or the "wisdom weed", a drug outlawed as dangerous.

Taken together, all these religions constitute a community of faith. Exposed to and influenced by this community from birth, no Jamaican is able, consciously, to resist its great moral stabilizing influence and its promise of a compensating good time in the life after death. It gives him a fine sense of right and wrong, of good and evil , of justice and injustice, of God and the Devil.

The part played by the churches, notably the Baptists in the grim days of slavery and the difficult post-emancipation period, particularly in their efforts to establish primary education and aid the ex-slaves in obtaining land atoned in great measure for the great sin of slavery.

Tombstones of those early missionaries crumbling in church graveyards all over the island, bear testimony to the solid Christian foundations they laid. So do four of the island's leading teacher training colleges.

Some of the new religions have banded into the Jamaica Association of Evangelical Churches, while most of the longer established ones are linked to the once powerful Jamaica Council of Churches.

The head of the Anglican Church is still titled the Lord Bishop of Jamaica (as in colonial times), while the head of the Roman Catholic

Church is titled the Archbishop. All the churches are as Jamaicanized as they will ever be with the sole exception of the Salvation Army, which still has a foreign head. In the past, the Lord Bishop opened Parliament with prayers. In independent Jamaica, the honour rotates among all the recognized orthodox religions.

The first Catholic Church in Seville, St. Ann parish, was built around 1510. Destroyed by fire, it was rebuilt and again went up in flames.

Believed to be jinxed , the site was abandoned but several more attempts were made elsewhere. The present church was completed as recently as 1924 by Fr. Raymond Sullivan, an energetic Jesuit, and figures pivotally in a joint project by the Jamaican and Spanish governments to unearth and preserve the historic Spanish ruins and artifacts in that area.

Holy Trinity Roman Catholic Cathedral, North Street

School girls walking home in the rain

St. Hilda's High School

A child, writing intently

University of Technology (UTECH) front wall

EDUCATION

Education is Jamaica's biggest, most expensive, most complex and most urgent exercise in national development. The government regards it as nothing less and gives it a high priorty rating. Evidence: every year Education receives one of the biggest slices of the national budget.

It isn't that Jamaica hopes to outstrip, in the forseeable future, the problems of providing adequate and meaningful education for all its population. In an island with a population that has grown by one million in the past thirty years, the problem cannot be outstripped without a considerable slowdown of the birth rate. However, there can be no reduction in financial outlay and physical effort. Whatever its problems (money, buildings, equipment, personnel), the system must cope with them somehow.

English and Scottish missionaries started education among the ex-slaves. Under tremendous handicaps and hardships, they found primary schools offering the basic "three R's" to help redress the imbalance of a colonial system which condemned the majority black population to be "hewers of wood and drawers of water" for the privileged and wealthy white and light-skinned minority.

The Jamaican government of the mid-fifties, then headed by the late Norman W. Manley, started opening the doors of the snob-ridden, elite high schools and colleges to the children of the masses, a process which was given further impetus by the late Edwin Allen, in his role as Minister of Education. Today, primary and secondary education are compulsory and free.

Ranging from simply primary to complicated and expensive technical, vocational and secondary education

The Mico University College

The Thomas Manning Building at Mannings High School

School children hard at work

scattered throughtout the island, the system must produce the vast recurring army of trained teachers needed in every area .

The long-standing Common Entrance Exam (or 11+) was sat for the last time in 1998, and students are now assessed for readiness for high school through the Grade 6 Achievement Test (GSAT).

At its upper levels, it must provide spring-boards to the higher echelons of technology, into medicine, law, teaching, social welfare, nursing and the public service, into engineering, agriculture and the arts and sciences.

Human Employment and Resource Training (HEART), started in 1983, assists in post-secondary training and skills development, as well as job placements for school leavers through public and private sector cooperation.

The Jamaica Foundation for Lifelong Learning (JFLL), began as Jamaica Movement for the Advancement of Literacy in 1973. Over the years its policies have been revamped and transformed into a lifelong learning organization that is in keeping with global standards and demands. The organization also supports the UNESCO (EFA) goal of basic education for all by 2015. They operate under the concept that "it's never too soon or too late to acquire and use knowledge to improve the quality of one's life."

The Ministry of Education introduced the Career Advancement Programme (CAP) in 2010 in partnership with the Jamaica Foundation for Lifelong Learning (JFLL), Heart Trust/NTA and the National Youth Service (NYS) to ensure that students who were graduating from high schools were both literate and numerate. They did this to ensure that the students would have some kind of vocational/technical qualification for post secondary studies or work.

The regionally run University of the West Indies (U.W.I.) was founded in 1948, shortly after World War II. It is located in a scenic setting at Mona (site of a slave-era sugar plantation), on the west bank of the Hope River, in St. Andrew.

The U.W.I. has three campuses: Mona (Jamaica), Cave Hill (Barbados) and St. Augustine (Trinidad). Its faculties are Agriculture, Humanities and Education, Engineering, Law, Medical Science, Pure and Applied Sciences and Social Sciences. Formerly a satellite college of London University, the U.W.I, has been autonomous since 1962.

Other tertiary institutions include the University of Technology (UTECH), which was formerly the College of Arts, Science and Technology (CAST), UTECH was granted university status in 1995 and offers technical and business courses and recently a Law programme. There is also the Edna Manley College of the Visual and Performing Arts, the College of Argriculture Science and Education (CASE), and several teacher-training institutions. Also included is the Northern Caribbean University (NCU), formerly West Indies College (WIC), which was granted University status in 1999 and offers degrees in a wide range of faculties.

Phillip Sherlock statue on the grounds of the University of the West Indies

TWO OUTSTANDING EDUCATORS

Civilized countries venerate their great men. For Aston Wesley Powell, M.A., B.Sc., Jamaica has done no less. A slim, quiet, self-effacing visionary and innovator, Powell, in 50 untrumpeted years, built the once inauspicious five-student Excelsior School into Excelsior Education Centre (EXED). Today the college has two major campuses (Mountain View and Camp Road) and provides numerous Bachelors, Associated Bachelors and certificate programmes.

Not the most prestigious, but perhaps the most eloquent award conferred on Wesley Powell, were the 1970 (N.Y.) Progressive League's award for "Outstanding Contribution to Jamaica in the field of Education", and the 1971 Award for Excellence by the Norman Manley Awards Committee.

"For Excellence" spells out the quality of his contribution in five decades of single-minded, inspired and original service.

With keen insight and an astute awareness of the human development needs of the West Indies region, Powell designed and gradually developed a post-primary to pre-university curriculum, which balanced academic and technical education, with ample attention to physical development, which became a model for developing countries.

Concurrently, he held office as chairman, director or member in 28 local and regional organizations as diverse as publishing, theology and the Jamaica Honours Awards Committee. Powell thanked the Methodist Church of Jamaica for their long and fruitful partnership with his ambition. The Methodists extol him for having invited them to join in an experiment that has become a solid, monumental accomplishment.

John James Mills (1888 – 1966). The common man who became "prince of Jamaican Educators". Few of todays senior generation can recall a time when the name John Mills was not synonymous with the Mico Teacher's College (now The Mico University College).

Brilliant student and tutor, peerless lecturer, historian and Bible scholar, Mills declined offers to higher and lucrative posts which would have separated him from the goal dearest to his heart, that of building character in his students while grooming them for careers as teachers and community leaders.

As tutor, father, friend, counsellor, confessor, he sent a total of 1,100 Miconians out to take their places in the schoolroom and the wider world. Many have ranked among the country's most brilliant headmasters. Others have moved into equally distinguished careers in politics, religion, agriculture, law, medicine, the civil service, and other notable fields in Jamaica and abroad.

His superlative students record at Mico is broken by only one man: the late Hon. Glen Owen, Privy Councilor to the Governor General and a past Mico Principal. Owen spoke of Mills' towering shadow as "the grandeur of a great mountain range".

John Mills died in 1966 and is buried in the cemetary of St. Andrew Parish Church in Half Way Tree. His monument is his imperishable, unsullied name, but an oak tree on Mico grounds will be more readily visible to tomorrow's generation, and more symbolic of the character of the man.

Top & bottom: Edna Manley College of the Visual and Performing Arts

WOMEN: THE FAMOUS, THE BEAUTEOUS & THE FABLULOUS

Jamaica probably has more women per thousand of population that any other country, irrespective of size. There is no field in which their numbers are not abundant and ever increasing. The arts, law, medicine, politics, education, social welfare, government, journalism, business, radio and television, and even transportation are fast becoming women's worlds.

Local anthropologists say it is the climate and the food which makes the women of this island unique in the world, that after over three centuries of free-wheeling miscegenation every Jamaican carries within him or her some of the seed of all the races that have mixed and melted into the mould of the creature called Jamaican, a creature who feels inferior to no one and often proves superior to many. In a word, there is no one like a Jamaican. No one hardier, more ingenious, more resilient or blessed with talent, good looks and vitality. There is no one more full of love and compassion; neither is anyone more quickly angered.

Their fashion-consciousness makes millionaires of traders in wearing apparel and cosmetics, and they keep an estimated 3,500 beauty parlors busy 365 days a year (as well as on the extra day in a leap year).

Every gathering of Jamaican women is a gathering of beauty queens – crowned and uncrowned, both present and potential. Repeatedly, Jamaican contestants have either carried off the Miss World Crown or have been runners-up.

Since invading agriculture many years ago they have thrown dust in the faces of their male counterparts, and at management level (where agriculture is weakest)

are sure to outnumber them in time. Not only because there are more women than men, but because today's Jamaican woman – irresepective of class – is fired with an ambition to achieve success in a society of equal opportunity.

SOPHIA MAX-BROWN
Managing Director of MAXBROWN LTD. and Satori Resort and Spa

DAWN HENRY
Managing Director,
LMH Group of Companies

HER EXCELLENCY THE MOST HONOURABLE LADY ALLEN
Educator, Adult Nurse Practitioner and wife of Governor General of Jamaica

MARLENE MALAHOO FORTE
Senator, Attorney-at-law

JANET FAGAN
Director of Marketing & Sales, Buzzz Caribbean Lifestyle Magazine

DR. ANISSA HOLMES
Owner of Jamaica Cosmetic
Dental Services

NOVIA McDONALD-WHYTE
Senior Associate Editor &
Lifestyle Editor of the
Jamaica Observer

TRISHAUNA CLARKE
Model, Nurse

TAMI CHYNN
Recording Artiste

JENEIL WILLIAMS
International Fashion Model

Pulse Modeling Agency, founded in 1982 by Kingsley Cooper, was the first Caribbean modeling agency to unearth the beauty and talent of the region and export it to the world. Pulse models have graced the covers of or done editorial fashion layouts in all the major fashion magazines. Here are some of the talented beauties who have paved the way for the new generation.

ROMAE GORDON

NADINE WILLIS

KIMBERLY MAIS

ALTHEA NEIL

ARTS & ENTERTAINMENT

Potter at work

Dancehall party

Street art

An artist beside his painting

Jamaica's arts and craft date back to slavery. African slaves brought their craft skills with them, and their religious rituals had a high theatrical content. Their ritualistic dances, once taboo but never quite suppressed, have become part of the cultural mix of today's Jamaican dance, both on stage and off.

Slave music and dancing, derived largley from West Africa, was blended with British hymns and English folk music to produce a very typically Jamaican art form called Mento. The Jamaican Folk Singers, led by Dr. Olive Lewin, has captured for posterity and the world, the original songs, the oral tradition and the music of our ancestors. The group has performed in all major capitals of the world, providing a kaleidoscope of Jamaican rhythm, folklore and drama.

The late thirites heralded not only the new political consciousness, but also the beginnings of a vigorous movement in painting, sculpture, literature, dance and drama. Since then, these art forms have been encouraged by the Edna Manley College of the Visual and Performing Arts which encompasses the schools of Art, Music, Dance, and Drama. The collective experiences of the Jamaican people have found a lasting place in the cultural life of the island.

The late Edna Manley was outstanding in promoting the growth of painting and sculpture from very small beginnings. Albert Huie, Carl Abrahams, Ralph Campbell, Van Pitterson, Richard Daley, David Pottinger and Alvin Marriot struggled as most pioneer artists do, for recognition and even survival. The second generaton owe their rise in prominence to a national awakening that Jamaican art, in any language, is fine art.

Outside of the mainstream, there have always been a number of self-taught artists; John Dunkley, Mallica "Kapo" Reynolds (who was also a revivalist and sculptor) and Sydney McLaren have gained international fame through the simplicity and clear freshness of their primitives. Cecil Baugh takes pride of place among the Master Potters of the world.

Today, Jamaica boasts an extensive National Art Gallery and an abundance of private galleries, open year round, to exhibit the talents of our artists.

National Gallery of Jamaica

The Little Theatre Movement (LTM), founded in 1941, is the oldest theatre group on the island. In its early beginnings, it was known for its production of the annual pantomime, which owes its "Jamaicanization" to the efforts of the late Greta Fowler and her husband, Henry. The pantomime, which opens every Boxing Day (December 26), celebrates Jamaican folklore and is a show-case for the talents of directors, choreographers, musicians, singers, dancers and actors. It is also a school of learning for a host of theatre technicians.

Other theatre groups, offer an eclectic choice ranging from risqué comedies to tried and tested international classics.

More recently, the talents of Jamaicans have been exposed to the wider world through the medium of feature films and television commercials, which have been produced here. Some films, which have used our production crews as well as actors, are "Clara's Heart", "Cocktail", "Lord of the Files", "The Mighty Quinn", and "Klash". A quarter of the crew and half of the cast of 40 in "The Mighty Quinn" was made up of Jamaicans. In the last fifteen years, the Jamaican film industry has really come alive with a number of films that have made it to the big screens. A few of these are: Third World Cop (1999); Shottas (2002); Glory to Gloriana (2006); Better Mus Come (2010); and Ghetta Life (2011). But this is merley a resurgence of earlier film activity, of which the Jamaican-made Perry Henzell film "The Harder They Come" is an international classic. Indeed, our own Trevor Rhone won a Canadian Oscar for his film "Milk and Honey".

Dance finds its excellence in the work of the National Dance Theatre Company (NDTC), which was formed in 1962 by its artistic director Professor, The Hon. Rex Nettleford, O.M., and its co-founder, Eddy Thomas. The NDTC has won international acclaim through its foreign tours; its annual season provides the core of its work, which is original, indigenous and exciting.

Much of Jamaican art, song and music are highlighted each year during the government-sponsored National Festival, as part of the country's annual independence celebrations. The Festival takes first place as a national, spiritual unifying force, transcending religious and political barriers in every area of arts, crafts and literature.

Jamaican Literature is as vibrant as it has ever been, with new writers making their mark in fiction- Colleen Smith-Dennis debut 'Inner City Girl' was nominated for the 2011 IMPAC Dublin Literary Award and Marlon James first novel, 'John Crow's Devil' released in 2005, was short-listed for the Commonwealth Writers' Prize and was a finalist for the Los Angeles Times Book Prize. Other writers making a huge impact are K.Sean Harris, one of the most prolific authors the region has ever seen having written over sixteen novels; Diana McCaulay, who has received critical acclaim for her debut novel 'Dog Heart' and Amanda Hannah, who has authored three Amazon Kindle bestsellers. Jamaica is also home to Calabash, the hugely popular and only literary festival in the Caribbean. Held at Jakes, in Treasure Beach, St. Elizabeth, the three- day festival was founded in 2001 and was back in 2012 after a one year hiatus in 2011.

A thriving publishing industry exists in Jamaica with many small, medium-sized and large publishers producing a wide variety of quality literature.

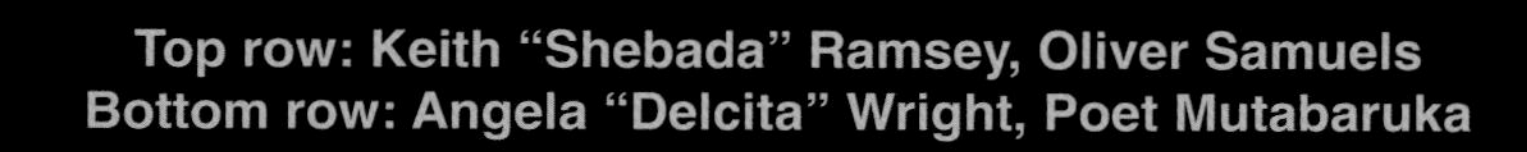

Top row: Keith “Shebada” Ramsey, Oliver Samuels
Bottom row: Angela “Delcita” Wright, Poet Mutabaruka

Jamaican craftwork, using local materials, is artistic, useful and colorful. Training is nurtured by the government agency, Things Jamaican and items of the highest standards are made available to visitors as well as to locals. An estimated of 40,000 persons are engaged in craft production.

A Tribute to Two Musical Greats

Gregory Isaacs

Gregory Isaacs dubbed the "Cool Ruler", was one of Jamaica's most talented reggae icons. He was born on July 15, 1951. Known for his sultry, cool and melodic voice, the "Cool Ruler" had a career that spanned over forty years.

From early on Gregory knew he had a passion for music. He recorded his first song "Another Heartache" in the late sixties. Though it was not a success, Isaacs held on to his dream of becoming a musician by forming a group called "The Concords" with Penro Bramwell. Even though they made a number of songs together, he still did not get a hit. This propelled him to go solo again.

Throughout the seventies, he dropped a number of songs for different record labels, even creating African Museum Record Label with his friend, another singer, Errol Dunkley. Songs such as: "I Need Your Loving", "Love is Overdue" and "Extra Classic", amongst others, were a part of this era. In 1978, he gained street credit when he created the album "Cool Ruler".

By the 1980's Gregory became one of the most eclectic and prolific reggae artiste in Jamaica. He produced his international hit "Night Nurse", which was also the name of his album. It climbed to number 32 on the British Charts. This song was loved for its cheeky title, sultry lyrics and sexual undertone.

Though a smooth lover's rock reggae singer, he was no saint. He started to have legal troubles as soon as his career started to peak. It did affect his career somewhat; however, this rude boy remained loved by his many fans, both locally and internationally. He continued singing throughout the decades dropping "Rumours" which was an instant hit in

1998. Though the nineties was the era of dancehall, Isaacs was still creating waves.

His last album in 2008 was called "Brand New Me." Sadly, the "Cool Ruler" passed away on October 25, 2010 of lung cancer. He is missed by his family and adoring fans all over the world.

Alton Ellis

Alton Nehemiah Ellis, OD, (September 1, 1938 – October 10, 2008) was a musician best known as one of the innovators of rock-steady music and was often referred to as the "Godfather of Reggae and the King of Rock-steady". Born in a musical family, he learned to play the piano at a young age but began his career as a dancer at the age of sixteen. After achieving many awards in this field over a two year period, Ellis took an interest in singing. His debut was as a vocal duo named Alton and Eddy. Their first recording on the Coxsone label, 'Muriel', was a major hit in Jamaican recording history. After Eddy left Jamaica to live in America, Alton formed a group named 'Alton and The Flames'. They recorded a large number of hit songs on the Treasure Isle label, including 'Dance Crashers', 'Girl I've got a Date', 'Rock Steady' and 'Black Mans Pride'. After three years with Alton and The Flames, Alton launched his career as a solo artist and joined the 'Studio One Label' in 1967. He created a huge number of hits during this period, including 'I'm Still in Love', 'Breaking Up' and 'I'm Just a Guy'. His album 'Rock and Soul', released on the Studio One label was groundbreaking, paving the way for the many that were to follow over the years. Alton left Jamaica in 1969 to spend two years in Toronto, Canada. He returned home for a period of three years and left again in 1974 to make his permanent home in London, England. Alton has worked with every significant artist in the Reggae field, he has taught many up-coming artists. In 2006, he was inducted into the International Reggae and World Music Awards Hall Of Fame.

Top row: Bounty Killer, Big Youth, Queen Ifrica, Shaggy
Bottom row: Cecile, Capleton, Julian Marley

Top row: Beenie Man, Buju Banton, Dennis Brown, Damion “Jr. Gong” Marley
Bottom row: Lady Saw, Tarrus Riley, Etana

"A Jamaican Athlete"

The Young Reggae Boyz in action

Kim Marie Spence, Women's Antarctic Expedition

The Sunshine Girls in action

NATION AT PLAY

Where there are fun and games, there you'll find Jamaicans; generating the action or enjoying it from the sidelines. Though there are thousands who work six or even seven days a week, for long periods without a break, there is a long held suspicion among employers that if Jamaicans had their way, a one-day work week would suit them fine, with five days for play and one for sleep!

Jamaicans boast a proud history for outstanding achievements in international sporting events, which have been recorded for posterity in a Hall of Fame. They excel in nearly every sport including swimming, lawn and table tennis, squash, field hockey, cycling, weight lifting, motor racing and track and field.

Our Olympic medalists include Arthur Wint, Herb Mckenley, Donald Quarrie, Merlene Ottey, Deon Hemmings, Grace Jackson Small, Juliet Cutbert, Veronica Campbell Brown, Asafa Powell, and Usain Bolt, among others.

Jamaica did very well at the 2008 Beijing Olympics. At the end of the events, Jamaica was fourth on the placing table with six gold, three silver and two bronze medals.

The London 2012 Olympics was a special one for Jamaica. In our 50th year of Independence, our athletes had a glorious opportunity to shine on the world stage in the nation from which Jamaica gained independence. They did not disappoint. With Usain Bolt leading the way by becoming the first athlete in history to win the sprint double at back to back Olympics, the

“A Jamaican Athlete”: a sculpture by
Alvin Marirott at the National Stadium

Jamaican athletes excelled, from Alia Atkinson's fourth place finish in the women's 100m breast stroke final, to Shelly-Ann Fraser-Pryce becoming the third woman in history to successfully defend the 100m title to Jamaica's historic 1-2-3 finish in the 200m men's final, they gave Jamaica a wonderful 50th anniversary present.

Boston Beach in the parish of Portland was Jamaica's first internationally recognized surf spot. Visitors to the famous beach witnessed local fishermen returning from sea and "surfing" their boats in on the powerful driving surf rolling into the cove and took the news back to eager ears. Surfers returned to ride the waves and when these surfers went home, they would sometimes leave their boards with locals and thus began the Jamaican surf story. Jamaica has a national surf team and outstanding surfer, Icah Wilmot, a regular fixture on the team, is a 4 time National Junior Champion and 5 time National Open Champ.

Jamaicans who have held world boxing titles are Micheal McCallum, Trevor Berbick, Lennox Lewis, Lloyd Honeyghan and Simon Brown.

Interestingly, this snowless island in the sun fielded a bobsled team for the first time in 1988 Calgary Winter Olympics and since then in 1992, 1994 and 1998. They acquitted themselves creditably and their courage and spirited determination made them crowd favourites every time. An internationally acclaimed movie, "Cool Runnings" has been made based on their story.

Not to be outdone, Jamaican netballers are ranked fourth in the world. The Jamaican national team is commonly referred to as the

Icah Wilmot in action

REEF

Top & bottom: Georgina Sergeon, Jamaica's lone female jockey

Sunshine Girls and the team is coached by former representative Oberon Pitterson-Nattie. Netball is the number one women's sport in Jamaica.

Despite the sedate pace of cricket, it can engender vociferous emotions among its spectators, as an English Test side learned in one game in Kingston, when a favorite batsman was called out. 2011 was a historic year for the national senior cricket team. The Tamar-Lambert led team won the West Indies Cricket Board (WICB) regional title for a fourth straight year to equal the feat accomplished by Barbados in the late 1970s.

The island has become a prime location for international golfing events. Its attractive and challenging courses meet the highest international standards and have hosted such pro greats as Chi-Chi Rodriquez and Nancy Lopez.

Horse racing in Jamaica is a male dominated sport and Georgina Sergeon is Jamaica's lone female jockey. She started riding as an apprentice in 2009 and she has ridden 55 winners, 25 of which were in her first full season at the Caymanas Park. In 2010, she was nominated for Jamaica's Sportswoman of the Year Award. She was injured in 2012 when her mount went down on a crowded field and she suffered injuries to her back and spine. It remains to be seen whether she will be able to ride again.

The island also has a full-sized motor racetrack at Dover Raceway in the hills overlooking Discovery Bay. This spectacularly

Jamaican bobsled team

sited raceway has attracted the attention of the international motor racing circuit and future plans include the building of a cycle track to international competition standards.

The Jamaica national football team, popularly known as the 'Reggae Boys', made history in 1998 by becoming the first English-speaking Caribbean country to qualify for the World Cup.

Jamaica is also the arena for world-class polo, regattas, marlin tournaments and even hot-air ballooning. The National Stadium in Kingston (capacity 30,000) was officially opened in August 1962, in time to celebrate Jamaica's Independence. Together with the adjoining National Arena, an indoor venue, they have afforded many local athletes their first taste of international competition.

Nearly every Government department, community and company has a sports club or team of some sort. Numerous clubs accommodate thousands of young and not-so-young men, women and children, burning up energy on indoor and outdoor tracks, courts and playing fields. Numerous gyms and health studios are now meeting the demands of the urban health conscious young professionals.

At any time of the year there are so many competitions going on, a computer would be hard put to keep track of them. Question: When do Jamaicans get work done? Answer: In between play times!

A debate has been raging for years about allowing casinos on the island. Those who are fearful of the aspects of gambling are losing ground to the others who argue that most tourist venues worldwide offer the entertainment of casinos.

The economic benefits that can be accrued from allowing casinos were the deciding factor in this debate. The Casino Gaming Act 2010 was passed to facilitate and regulate the casino industry.

There is also a booming Lottery industry with different games being played throughout the day and on various days throughout the week, except on Sundays and public holidays. Some proceeds from the lottery go towards funding sports in the island through the Sports Development Foundation.

Meanwhile, behind closed doors of exclusive clubs and north coast hotels, there are gambling actions a plenty, night and day, in and out of season. For most humans, gambling is second nature and therefore irrepressible.

TOURISM

Sun, sand, sea, scenery and hospitality are intrinsic components of Jamaica's tourist trade. Nature lays on the first four lavishly; the fifth comes naturally – and as lavishly – from the people. This is the combination of fortunate circumstances that makes tourism Jamaica's largest industry. The government spends millions each year to promote it as a product. Private interests (hotels, guests houses, air and land transport services) spend even more in individual and joint efforts to woo visitors to sample the product.

Fern Gully, St. Ann

Farquhar's Beach (black sand), Clarendon

Black River Safari, St. Elizabeth

Bridge at Rockhouse Hotel, Negril

Ocho Rios, St. Ann

Ian Flemming Airport, St. Mary

A view of Ocho Rios, St. Ann

Top & bottom: YS Falls, St. Elizabeth

The Early Years

Capt. L. D. Baker, an enterprising Bostonian, initiated the banana and tourist trades simultaneously, each complementing the other as a money earner for him. His ships carried bananas from Port Antonio to Boston and paying passengers on the southward run. The early visitors came curiously to see how big a storyteller Baker was and whether his picture of the island was overstated.

But Baker had not told the romantic half. Year after year his boats, identifiable by the red diamond on their white funnels, arrived in Port Antonio and later Kingston, laden with sun seekers who had been told by previous visitors that Jamaica was indeed what Baker said – and much more.

Realizing that he was on to a good thing, Baker built a hotel, the Titchfield, near his banana wharf at Port Antonio, for the comfort of the vistors he brought. As they fanned out to see more of the island, he built another, the Myrtle Bank, in Kingston.

The message of a big new trade in the making reached St. James parish in the west. Mrs. Ethel Hart, a prominent citizen with a keen business eye, built a palatial wooden place on a hill atop Montego Bay and named it Ethelhart Hotel. Ma Ewen, in the same mould, rechristened her white-framed guest-house, on the shoreline close by, Casa Blanca. Dr. McCatty, a keen sea bather, discovered that the water near the Casa Blanca did something marvelous to a man other than cool his body on a hot summer's day. Thus was Doctor's Cave born, destined to become one of the travel world's most famous beaches.

Bahia Manteca, the little country port which Spaniards had built as a convenient spot for shipping manteca (lard), began to come alive to the possibilities of tourism.

Anticipating the swelling inflow of North Americans and Britons, the government set up a Tourist Trade Development Board in Kingston. But it was not until the mid-30s that tourism began to assume larger-than life, glamorous proportions with hotels popping up along the whole northern coastline like lilies at Easter time.

In the mid-50s, a brash, freckled-faced young Montegonian, John Pringle, pioneered the ritzy resort west of the town which he called Round Hill and, in a feat of salesmanship never before seen in Jamaica, enticed plane-loads of North America's most fabulous, rich and famous jet setters (including a young Senator named John F. Kennedy) to come and enjoy the action.

Against all advice, a dry goods merchant named Abe Issa built a catering palace near Ocho Rios. He called it Tower Isle, after the islet offshore on which he built a miniature tower. Today it is known as Couples and it is mostly always full of happy vacationing couples. Soon he had plenty of company east and west of him.

In the "cradle of tourism", Port Antonio, Ma and Pa Arnett meanwhile were adding more rooms to their guest house atop Bonnie View Hill. Four miles further along the coast road, biscuit millionaire, Grainger Weston built a super-exclusive resort in a storybook setting, naming it after the sheltered cove at its front door, Frenchman's Cove.

Some of the world's biggests and most magnificent cruise ships made Jamaica a must stop. The Palisadoes peninsula sprouted an international airport near the old pirate's play-ground, Port Royal, and Montego Bay built another for the planes that brought the flocks of human migratory birds south to sunshine each winter.

Baker's Myrtle Bank, demolished years ago to make way for Kingston's waterfront

Tourist playing with dolphins at Dolphin Cove, St. Ann

Rafting on the Rio Grande, Port Antonio

Jamaica, at its unique best

Boys having fun

Top: Inside the Green Grotto Caves, St. Ann
Bottom: Rockhouse Hotel, Negril

development, became famous as the "Gateway to Jamaica". In time, Kingston, like Montego Bay and the north coast, had its flowering of new and now well-known hotels to share the boom.

The '70s Onwards

A gradual decline set in, as Jamaica, under Micheal Manley began to make big, bad headlines in the foreign press. The result was a massive loss in revenues for all the hotels. To save many hotels from closing – actually to preserve the workers' jobs – the government stepped in, bailing out a round dozen, either wholly or partially buying them out, and kept them open. But the headlines became worse and the trade went elsewhere.

A change was due, and it came in the shape of a new Prime Minister, Edward Seaga, and with him came new economic policies. The government began putting its house in order, stabilizing the economy and clearing up Jamaica's image abroad. They unloaded the hotels, leasing them to private enterprise, which took up the challenge to halt the decline and turn the trade around.

This period saw the birth of the all-inclusive hotels, based on the overwhelmingly successful Club Mediterranean concept. It spawned the growth of two highly successful all-inclusive chains. The first was Superclubs, run by a trio of dynamic hoteliers, John Issa and his former partners, Frank Rance and Tony Ferrari, and then came Sandals Resorts owned and run by the dynamic Gordon "Butch" Stewart.

As private enterprise responded to the challenge of revitalizing the industry, other entrepreneurs jumped on the bandwagon. Following the prevailing trend towards fitness which continues to sweep the western world, some hotels – such as Sans Souci – upgraded and restyled their accommodation to provide health spas, complete with jacuzzis, hot tubs, gyms and tailored fitness programs.

By 1987, Jamaica was again benefiting from a healthy increase in visitors, surpassing the one million mark. This was repeated in 1988, although overseas publicity of damage following Hurricane Gilbert's passage through the island managed to sabotage some of the trade's best efforts.

In the years since Gilbert, the industry has enjoyed fairly consistent growth and in the year 2002, despite 9/11, Jamaica saw an expansion and growth with gross earnings amounting to $1209 million U.S. dollars. The boom in tourism on the north coast is now complimented by the development in other parts of the island.

South Coast: This area stretches from Old Harbour Bay through May Pen, including Milk River, and Mandeville, and has seen the rise of such attractions as the Black River Safari; the Treasure Beach areas which boasts Jakes, the home of the Calabash Literary Festival; and Beaches Hotel in south eastern Westmoreland, all of which is enhanced by Jamaica's first toll road from Portmore in St. Catherine, via the South Coast and through rugged Cockpit Country to the North Coast.

Negril: Hedonistic, laid-back, "Tahiti of the Caribbean", Negrillo, as the Spaniards named it, lies in the parish of Westmoreland and extends from the western end of the horse-shoe-shaped Bloody Bay, to the gently curving Long Bay including the extreme western tip of the island. It was once part of a great morass or swamp, much of which has been drained to provide the developed areas behind the beach. Fragments of the morass remain intact, jealously guarded by naturalists for whom it

Holland Bamboo, St. Elizabeth

Top: Bobsled ride down Mystic Mountain, St. Ann
Bottom: Negril Sunset

Top: Sea stacks at Long Road, Portland
Bottom: Dunns River Falls, St. Ann

holds interesting wild life and remnants of the original swampy forests.

Negril laid untouched, a sleepy backwater until 1969, its one notable hotel, the Sundowner, and a sprinkling of rustic guesthouses, the only accommodation. First came the hippies, the "flower children" of the 60s, hanging out on the beach, cooling out under the thatched roof, the pungent smell of ganja (marijuana) redolent in the air. Then a new breed of well heeled, mostly young American visitors began to follow their noses. Overnight , Negril became the most action-packed corner of the island.

The boom created a surge in building to accommodate the overflow from the old guest houses such as The Sundowner, Negril Beach Villas, Coconut Grove, and T-water Cottages, to name a few. Along came Buxton Cooke, a Jamaican with a B.Sc., in Agriculture and a Masters in Finance. He was the first "outsider" to accurately see Negril's long-term prospects as a resort area and together with his wife Mabel, he built Villas-Negril, a 19-villa complex of 46 bedrooms on a rocky promontory over-looking the seven-mile-long beach. This was soon followed by others such as Hedonism II, Sandals (Negril), Grand Lido and now Beaches, the latest addition to the Sandals chain of all-inclusive resorts.

In the wake of this boom came a never-ending cornucopia of restaurants, cafes, bars, souvenir and T-shirt stands. Negril continued to thrive through the 70s when other resorts along the coast and inland were experiencing lean times. Though there are some who can recall when Negril did not even have telephone lines, today there is even an airstrip.

Negril may well become Jamaica's first authentic nudist colony. Add abundant seafood, snorkling and sailing, diverse entertainment, a free-flowing torrent of wine in the hotels, sleek saddle horses and woodland trails, excursions to Booby Cay just a mile offshore, and what do you have? A heady, hedonistic exoticism, which not even Tahiti can beat. Since then, Negril has welcomed the arrival of the giant Spanish Hotel chain RIU.

Montego Bay, fifteen minutes by jet from Kingston or 3½ – 4 hours by road, via Fern Gully to Ocho Rios and along the coast road. Montego Bay ("MoBay" locally) is Jamaica's second city and premier resort. Montegonians used to call it "the Republic" to signify how different it is – and they are – from the rest of Jamaica.

It has reasons to consider itself special. Until recently, more dollar millionaires and blue-blooded Britons could be found floating around Montego Bay than perhaps in Nassau. There are the fine first families whose names, wealth and leadership can be traced three or four generations back. Montego Bay is proud of its service and civic clubs, its lively Chamber of Commerce, its hotel association, all actively dedicated to the proposition that their town is a place apart from all other places, bar none, and no two ways about it.

The town in which Dr. McCatty discovered his therapeutic Doctor's Cave Beach, has been transformed into high-rise hotel clusters. Even the Bogue islands, a small group of offshore cays, have been joined to the mainland to form Montego Freeport with holiday villas and hotels. With the best sailing conditions in the islands, regattas are often held over here, the highlight of the year being the Miami-Montego Bay Yacht Race, an international event. The addition of the Ritz Carlton and the expansion of the Sangster International Airport to accommodate Air Jamaicas' hub (now Caribbean Airlines), speaks to the future and all it holds for Jamaica.

Top: Tourists and locals frolicking in a river
Bottom: Cane River Falls, St. Andrew

Ocho Rios, a corruption of the Spanish "Los Chorreras", meaning sprouts or waterfalls. This whole stretch of coastline was once covered by a series of rivers, which gushed out of limestone rocks, forming spectacular cascades. Today, the only one of those falls not harnessed for electricity or water supply is Dunns River Falls, still one of Jamaica's best-known attractions.

Ocho Rios has long ceased to be just a simple fishing village and pirate hangout. More relaxed than Montego Bay, yet not as a laid-back as Negril, the town is bursting at the seams, a bustling, vibrant place with hotels and villas to walk about. Ocho Rios is also home to some of Jamaica's most beautiful attractions. Places such as White River, Mystic Mountains, Dolphin Cove and James Bond Beach, make Ocho Rios worth visiting. It is centrally located on the island; roughly halfway between Montego Bay and Port Antonio, and a mere 1 1/2 hours drive from Kingston. Ocho Rios is the fastest growing town on the north coast today.

Port Antonio, with its twin habours and Navy Island guarding the approaches, occupies the most beautiful site of any small town in Jamaica. The boom days of the banana trade when the harbours were busy night and day are but an echo now, but the town still has a reputation as the hideout of the rich and famous. There are hotels like Frenchman's Cove and the most recent but well-known Trident Hotel, the resting place of choice for visiting film stars and European gentry. Port Antonio is one of the best centres for water sports in Jamaica as some of the best snorkeling and scuba diving in Jamaican waters is off these shores. The annual Marlin Tournament in October is an international event and during the tournament, the town comes alive again.

Home to many international figures such as the late Errol Flynn and Noel Coward, it is also the site for a unique Jamaican adventure, river rafting on the Rio Grande, one of the major attractions for the north coast. The frail-looking bamboo rafts once carried heavy loads of bananas down to Port Antonio. Now they carry passengers on what must surely be one of the most spectacular scenic trips anywhere. The Rio Grande, rising some 3,000 feet up in the Blue Mountains is one the island's swiftest rivers, coursing through lush tropical vegetation overhanging the water's edge. A trip down this river is reminiscent of earlier days when Arawak Indians fished and swam here and the whole island lived up to its name, Xamayca, Land of wood and water.

All of this has now been complemented by the new Port Antonio Marina which is capable of docking up to 32 yachts; and also the staging of the 2002 Tall Ships Regatta billed as America Sails. Port Antonio is now a haven for yachtsmen of the world.

Eco-tourism is also developing in the island with visitors heading into the lush, hilly interior in search of nature trails, horseback riding and the unspoiled wetlands.

Jamaica's rich musical heritage is also a part of the island's appeal to visitors from around the world. Annual events like the Jamaica Jazz & Blues Festival, Reggae Sumfest and Rebel Salute are well attended by people from all corners of the globe. Jamaica is also a source of inspiration for artistes who want to record new material in a different setting. Popular recording artistes like Rihanna, Amy Winehouse, Drake and Santigold have all recorded songs in Jamaica.

PARKS & BOTANICAL GARDENS

Anthurium

Hibiscus

"Garden Island" are rapturous words that spring from the lips at the sight of Jamaica's all year floral abundance. Giant bouquets of flaming Poinciana and gold Cassia Fistula rise against summer's azure sky. Yellow Poui petals carpet the grass. At eye level, Indian Lilac – often called "June Rose" – exudes soft perfume from crinkled flowers whose white and pastel seem strangely modest among the clash of primary colors.

From late August through October, the midnight opening (with an audible "phit") of Jamaica's largests blossom, the powerfully scented Cereus is a never-to-be-forgotten spectacle, so completely expressive of nature's beauty that at sunrise these flowers die, as if to attest that their beauty is literally unbearable.

Following Jamaica's rainy season, the land takes on a vibrant glow manifested in a kaleidoscope of colourful plants and flowers; Brunfelsia's waxen cream trusses and starry white jasmine; Crinum, growing in bunches of as many as a dozen on a single stem while the variously named Spider Lily and Candy Lily exude a sweetness, which pervades the air. Small, so-called Rain Lilies, known as Jamaican Crocus – yellow, pink, mauve, white – seemingly dance in the wet wind that blows across pasture lands.

Jamaica's December blossoms create a giant Christmas card, as the pure white Euphorbia (leucocephalia-lotsy), in rounded hillocks, is surrounded by related scarlet Euphorbia (poinsettia). Together they dramatize the convention of white and red Christmas colors symbolizing Christ's purity and His sacrifice.

Hope Gardens

Bougainvillea of myriad dark and light colors riot over hedges, many of hybrids yet unnamed by taxonomists who cannot keep pace with their mutations.

Who, looking at Jamaica's abundance of tropical blossoms, could expect to also see the rose achieve perfection as though in the protection of a northern garden? Yet the rose, above all, is the pride of the Jamaican nurseryman from whose hand comes the near-black Papa Meilland and the floribunda Queen Elizabeth in no less form, texture and total loveliness than in the countries where they were bred. In addition, Carnations, Pinks, Larkspur and Salvia ornament Jamaica's gardens in town and country. Competing for attention are Touch Gingers and Anthurium, while humming birds dip long beaks to sip from the recesses of the vivid Heliconia bracts. The beauty of the gardens are breath-taking.

It is not surprising that no one has ever contradicted a lecturer's statement to the Linnean Society that "Jamaica's flowering species are more than those of any land except Sri Lanka". In orchids alone, Jamaica numbers over 250 species, many endemic, some so small that their perfection is seen only with the mircoscope.

Much of Jamaica's plant catalogue is not native but instead is a credit to the British navy. This is a fact of history. The British, in their imperial years, set out in England park-like gardens to hold foreign plants ordered to be brought from colonies in South and Central America, Africa and India.

The sailing ship, however, was slow and its sailing time very often determined the plants' survival. So Jamaica, approximately midway in the Atlantic sea routes, was designated a stopover where fresh water was taken aboard for both the crew and the plants. It was also found that Jamaica's multiple mini-climates, ranging from arid flatlands to cold mountains, offered the ideal place to rest and restore those specimens that seemed affected by distance and travel. This ultimately led to the British intent that propagations might be made in Jamaica for later transfer to England.

HOPE
GARDENS

Emancipation Park, New Kingston

St. William Grant Park, Downtown, Kingston

An example of hope frustrated is Amhersita, a leguminous flowering tree standing at the lower gateway of Castleton Botonical Gardens, whose racemes of large salmon orchid-like flowers recall the exquisite Lady Amherst, wife of a former Governor of Burma, where the blooms are temple flowers. Amherstia survives in Jamaica, though still difficult to propagate and, to date, totally rejecting all efforts of the skilled experts at Kew, the Royal Botanica Gardens on the outskirts of London.

Jamaicas' preference among flower colours perhaps is blue, a truth emphasized in the choice of the national flower, the lignum vitae, a small, many-bunched, star-like bloom, smoky blue with a golden center.

Blue too is the plumbago grown in geometric beds of large gardens and flowering hedges of small suburban residences. The blue lily, spectacular of Mandeville is, for Jamaicans, what cherry blossoms viewing is to the Japanese. So all through April to June, Mandeville is thronged, as for a pilgrimage, to the blue Lily. For there is no greater balance to nature than the sight of the Caribbean's blue flowers against a backdrop of blue skies whose colors affirm that over the hill is the incredibly blue Caribbean Sea.

It is almost impossible to visit Jamaica and be unaware of the fauna or wildlife, particularly at night. The cacophony of sound produced by the small whistling frogs plays counterpoints to the chirping of the crickets, as soon as the sun dips below the horizon, producing a sometimes almost deafening concerto.

The whistling frog was first introduced to Jamaica in the 19th century by a governor's wife, Lady Blake, because she Liked the sound. From the grounds of King's House it has spread all over the island.

After iron, aluminium – the lightweight metal with a thousand uses – is modern man's most useful metal. Aluminium is made from alumina, which is made from bauxite. Mining the raw bauxite and processing it into alumina are, dually, very important sectors of the Jamaican economy. In 1997 the gross earnings from alumina and crude bauxite were US $661.41 million and US $71.13 million respectively.

Jamaica's bauxite, roughly speaking, occurs in a broad band running north to south across the island's middle. Largest deposits are in the parishes of St. Ann, Manchester, St. Elizabeth and Trelawny. Some smaller deposits exist in the parishes of Clarendon and St. Catherine, and there is bauxite in the highlands from about 1,200 feet above sea level, lying in pockets and bowls of limestone.

Bauxite is generally called "red dirt". But not all of Jamaica's bauxite is red or reddish brown, a peculiarity, which indicates not alumina, but iron mineral in the soil. There is no overburden covering the bauxite as is the case in many countries. The ore lies right on the surface, making Jamaican bauxite soft, easy and cheap to mine.

About half of Jamaican-mined bauxite is shipped raw to the U.S.A. The other half is processed in four alumina refineries with a combined capacity of some 2.7 million metric tons a year. The alumina is exported mainly to North America, Western Europe and Russia.

It takes about 2.5 tons of bauxite to produce one ton of alumina, which is a chemical bonding of alumina and oxygen. Two tons of alumina will produce one ton of aluminium.

Not until World War II created an increased demand for aluminium was much attention paid to the rich deposits of bauxite outside

Cinchona Botanical Gardens

Europe and the U.S.A. Bauxite was first discovered in Jamaica in 1942, on the property of the late Sir Alfred da Costa, Jamaican millionaire businessman. Three North-American companies-Aluminium Company of Canada (Alcan), Reynolds Mining Company and Kaiser Company-quickly acquired reserve lands, brought in mining machinery and built installations. By June 1952, when Reynolds became the first to start exporting from their port in Ocho Rios, the war had long been over, but the demand for aluminium continued. Kaiser followed suit a year later from a south coast port, which they built. Alcan built a processing plant near its Kirkvine (Manchester) mines and, in early '59, began shipping alumina, the intermediate product between ore and metal. The bauxite boom was on, just in time to shore up Jamaica's faltering sugar and banana economies.

In 1971, the island's fourth alumina plant was built at Maggoty, St. Elizabeth by Revere Copper and Brass. Two years later, Alcoa, which had been shipping raw bauxite since 1963, built the fifth refinery at Haise Hall, Clarendon. By 1974, Jamaica had become the world's fourth largest producer and second biggest alumina exporter.

No smelters have been built on the island, and it is unlikely that any will be because of two factors. Firstly, aluminium smelting requires massive electricity energy; hence smelters are usually sited where there is hydropower or coal. Jamaica gets its energy from imported petroleum and has no exploitable coal deposits. Secondly, smelters are usually located in countries with sizeable aluminium market.

The 1970s brought other changes to Jamaica's position in the world aluminium industry. In 1971, Australia overtook Jamaica as the world's top bauxite producer and there was increasingly stiff competition from other countries, notably Guinea, West Africa. Soaring oil prices in 1974 added to Jamaica's economic difficulties at a time when they could least afford it.

Although bauxite had been state-owned since colonial times, the companies had all been wholly owned subsidiaries of North American corporate parents. The result was that despite peak production of nearly 13 million tons of bauxite in 1973, for example, Jamaica's share of revenue was a mere US $35 million.

The government took several steps to redress the imbalance. First they slapped a production levy on the bauxite companies and then began buying into the local companies. The levy caused Revere to close their plant, complaining that operations had become uneconomical, but Jamiaca gained the major share in Kaiser and Reynolds, as well as an increased share of Alcoa and Alcan.

Third, the government repurchased most of the ore reserve lands but in return granted the companies long mining leases of those lands.

The 1980's saw a temporary take-over of Alcoa by the Government to form Clarendon Alumina Producers (CAP). Since then Alcoa has taken back half ownership in the plant. More recently Bauxite/Alumina Companies in Jamaica have been discussing the possibilites of expansion, which would further increase the country's output of bauxite, which in 1997 stood at 11,987.304 tons.

JAMAICAN CUISINE & COCKTAILS

Jamaican Cocktails

Prendyz on the Beach

Fried Lobster

It has taken a long time for the world to discover the delight of Jamaican food and drink. Food which reflects the reality of a land of exclusive spices, herbs and fruit; a country almost singularly producing the Pimento (Allspice); a land claiming the best ginger and coffee.

To enjoy Jamaican food, one must run the gamut from roadside eating of Boston jerk pork, jerk chicken, manish water, callaloo and curried goat, to the delight of a nouvelle course including Peanut Ginger Chicken or Ackee Quiche served in the setting of an exclusive hotel restaurant, previously the enclave of American and European cuisine.

In Jamaica, the local bar gives pride of place to one of the Jamaican male's most enjoyable past-times, that of drinking; whether it's the itinerant vendors' "roots" wine, Irish Moss, or the local bars mix of white rum and ginger beer, the Jamaican array of blends is equal to the best in the world.

Who can resist the lure of a cold Red Stripe Beer on a blistering hot day, or the smooth taste of Tia Maria Coffee Liqueur? The award-winning blends of Appleton rum are never far away, nor is the pleasure of a sip of Sangster's Rum Cream. To top off any meal with a cup of Jamaican Blue Mountain coffee is the epitome of gourmet dining.

Whether one chooses the roadside stop or the simple, yet totally Jamaican snack food, the ubiquitous "Tastee" patty or "Juici" patty, there is always more to be experienced and learned about Jamaican foods. Be it from the ital eating shops or not, you will truly find as, Bob Marley said, that you are "Coming in from the cold".

So taste and experience a culture of spicy, pungent food, hardly ever needing more than the stomach space for a second helping.

Jamaican Recipes

Reproduced from the book "Jamaican Cooking & Menus"

LMH PUBLISHING

RED PEAS SOUP

1 pint of red peas (soak overnight)
2 qrts. water
1 lb. soup meat
¼ lb. of pig's tail
1 sliced coco
1 minced onion
* salt, thyme, hot pepper to taste

Method:

1. Place peas and meats in water. Boil until peas are almost tender. Add coco and seasonings. When peas and coco are cooked, remove the meats.
2. Soup may be served with whole peas, or, put through a colander and discard skins. Small dumplings are usually added to this soup.

COCONUT DROPS

2 cups coconut, diced
1 teaspoon powdered ginger or
1 tablespoon root ginger
1 pinch of salt
1 teaspoon vanilla
1lb or 450g brown sugar
3 cups water

Method:

1. To dice, pry coconut from the shell with a knife.
2. Bring water to a boil and add all ingredients.
3. Boil for about 30 minutes (stir occasionally with a wooden spoon to keep sugar from binding) or until very sticky.
4. Remove by spoonfuls and drop onto a greased tin sheet. Cool and eat.

GRATER CAKE

2 cups grated coconut
1 lb/450g brown sugar
½ cup water
½ teaspoon ginger
* pinch of salt

Method:

1. Combine ingredients in a thick-bottomed saucepan.
2. Boil until coconut is cooked and the mixture is sticky enough to hold together.
3. Remove from heat and beat mixture for 2 to 3 minutes.
4. Shape into squares while still hot.
5. Allow to cool.

ESCOVEITCH OF FISH

- * small fish or slices of king fish
- * oil
- 1 cup vinegar
- 2 sliced onions
- 2 tablespoons water
- 1 chopped hot pepper
- * a pimento leaf and a pinch of salt

1. Fry fish in hot oil and set aside. Mix remaining ingredients together and bring to a boil. Simmer for about 20 minutes.
2. Lay fish in a shallow dish. Cover with hot vinegar sauce and marinate for about 12 hours before serving.

Curry Goat & Roti

Cheese cake at Susie's Bakery, Kingston

Bagel sandwich at Susie's Bakery, Kingston

Cream of Coconut Soup at South Beach Cafe, Kingston

Jerk Pit at 'Scotchies', Kingston

Top & Bottom: South Beach Cafe, Kingston

Jamaican Cocktails

Reproduced from Mike Henry's "Jamaican Cocktails & Mixed Drinks"

LMH PUBLISHING

GREEN PARROT

1 oz. Wray & Nephew White Overproof Rum
4 oz. orange juice
1 oz. Blue Curacao

Method:

- Pour ingredients one at a time, in the order listed above, into a large stemmed glass over ice. Do not mix. Garnish with an orange slice.

MONKEY'S UNCLE

2 parts Sangster's Jamaica Rum Cream
1 part Créme de Banana
1 part Appleton Estate VX Jamaica Rum

Method:

- Combine ingredients with cubed ice, shake and strain into martini glass.

NUTTY PROFESSOR

3 parts Sangster's Jamaica Rum Cream
1 part Frangelico hazelnut liqueur

Method:

- Combine all ingredients in a rock glass over ice.

ORANGE DAIQUIRI

1 ½ oz. Appleton Special Jamaica Rum
Juice of 1 orange
Juice of ¼ lime
1 oz sugar syrup
1 scoop crushed ice

Method:

- Mix all ingredients in blender, serve in a cocktail glass and garnish with orange slice.

V/X JAMAICAN COFFEE

1 ½ oz. Appleton Estate V/X Jamaican Rum
Hot black coffee
Splash of whipped cream

Method:

- Combine V/X and coffee in coffee mug.
- Top with whipped cream.

PATOIS & THINGS JAMAICAN

What language do Jamaicans speak? And how did they come to speak as they do?

These two questions are usually asked, at some stage, by strangers to the Caribbean and even English speaking visitors to the island. The answer is English – but not as you have heard it spoken anywhere else.

Consider the many nationals and cultures that have fused into a people who now call themselves Jamaicans, and you will have part of the answer. Despite standardization of schooling, Englishmen themselves (to say nothing of Welshmen, Irishmen and Scots) speak their language in countless variations. To remain alive, language must change and grow. As it is spoken in Jamaica, it is guaranteed to remain alive and well for quite some time.

Apart from newly coined words, there are mispronunciations and unusual applications of standard words: "Yu mean de likkle bwoy?" (Do you mean the little boy?), or "im jus' gawn fi a likkle while" or 'im soon come" is a misleading term. It means an infinite period of time anywhere from five minutes to an hour or more, as is "jus' roun' de corner" which could be next to where you are standing, or several miles away. To the average Jamaican, time and distance are not terribly significant.

Jamaica's cultural beliefs and practices also reflect their diverse origins. A popular proverb is "duppy know who fe frighten" i.e. do not provoke those who will retaliate. The word "duppy" means a ghost or spirit of

A little boy in earnest conversation with two donkeys.

Jamaica's famous 'pum pum' rock.

Wacky architecture.

The coolest dock you will ever see.

In other words, don't make one.

the dead. It is based on the African belief that man has two souls, one of which goes to heaven to be judged, while the other lingers on earth for a time or forever. The earth-bound spirit is either evil or good, depending on the character of the person while they lived.

The Jamaican quadrille shares some elements with the "square dance' of North America, both of them having originated with the European quadrille. Classical quadrille in Jamaica started out as a dance of the gentry, soon taken up by slaves who added their own touches. Quadrille has been handed down through the generations, and public performances are most often seen nowadays as part of the festival celebrations, produced annually to celebrate Jamaica's independence.

The same is true of May Pole dancing, a social dance originating in England as part of May Day celebrations. As with quadrille, it is most frequently performed as part of Festival.

Mento is Jamaica's best-known type of folk music, most commonly performed by small bands in north coast hotels, preferably poolside. Mento is a complete musical form as it refers not only to the music, but also to the words and dance particularly, with the influence of recorded music. The development of other popular Jamaican music styles such as Ska, Rock Steady and Reggae also spelled the decline of Mento, although its influence in these newer musical forms is strong.

Today, only a few Mento bands remain, defined by their traditional instruments: the rumba box, guitar and/or banjo, as well as shakers and graters. The origin of the word are lost in time but old timers regard Mento music with great nostalgia. For them, it was truly 'irie' music.

'Dutch' pots on a cotton tree trunk

Interesting roots

POPULAR JAMAICAN WORDS & PHRASES

Ah Nuh Nutten: No big deal; Unimportant.

Ah Yah So Nice: This is the place to be.

Bless: A form of greeting and it's also used to indicate that all is well.

Boots: Condom.

Bill: Relax; Calm down.

Cut Eye: To look at someone in a malicious manner.

Cutliss: Machete.

Dem: Them

Dread: Rastafarian.

Facety: Rude or disrespectful.

Fassy: Someone who is unreasonable or unfair.

Gallis: Male with many girlfriends

Ginnal: Con man or trickster

Gwaan: Go on

Jeezam: An expression used to convey surprise

Lawd: Lord.

Massa God: My God.

Mawga: Skinny.

Mo Fyah: More fire - an expression of excitement.

Nyam: Eat.

Rasta: Short for Rastafarian.

Unda Mi Nose: Right before my very eyes.

War Boat: A violent or quarrelsome person.

Why Pree?: Why are you watching me or why are you looking at me.

Zeen: Okay; That's cool.

KINGSTON: JEWEL OF THE CARIBBEAN

Tracks and Records, Kingston

Pan chicken man, Kingston

ob Marley Statue, Arthur Wint Drive, Kingston

Knutsford Boulevard, New Kingston

Port Royal's convulsive death by earthquake in 1692 sent survivors of the quake fleeing across the habour to start life anew in Kingston, then a small settlement on the edge of the vast mangrove swamp that bordered the Liguanea Plain leading up to Blue Mountains.

By 1703, Kingston was offically a town and the chief seat of trade. By 1801 the city's population had grown to 30,000: 9,000 whites, 4,000 free colored, 2,000 free blacks and 15,000 slaves. Only 250 persons – all white – had votes. This did not include women, Jews, colored or blacks who were vote-less.

It was the 250 who, under the Act of Incorporation in 1802, elected the first City Council (or Vestry) consisting of seven eldermen, seven councilmen and a chairing mayor.

Fires, earthquakes, droughts, storms, floods and diseases plagued the city. In 1849, Asiatic cholera alone killed 32,000. But Kingston refused to die, thriving on the wars that raged up and down the Spanish Main. In 1876 the six square mile town (which was also a parish) annexed the neighbouring and larger parish of St. Andrew, so as to have more space in its backyard. It also annexed Port Royal and the five-mile long Palisadoes peninsula. In 1872 Kingston was declared the capital of Jamaica replacing Spanish Town.

By 1900, the population numbered 55,000, minus Port Royal and Palisadoes, which had "seceded". Seven years later came the worst earthquake and fire that ever

Aerial view of the Half-Way-Tree Transport Centre

Knutsford Boulevard, New Kingston

Kingston at night on New Year's Eve

lit the city. It was a disguised blessing despite its terrible toll on life and property, for it necessitated rebuilding the ugly sprawling city with some semblance of order.

From there on, Kingston began to modernize its buildings (bricks largely replaced wood), water supply, sanitation and health services. Residents, vowing never again to be caught in a city that could quake and shake so much, began to spread out onto the plain beyond.

With continued growth and expansion, much of the original commercial activity, previously centred in downtown Kingston, moved uptown into New Kingston, leaving behind a forlorn assemblage of rundown buildings.

The waterfront developments of the Urban Development Corporation (UDC) have, in recent times, led to a modern set of high-rise buildings lining the waterfront. Also since the mid-1980s the Kingston Restoration Company (KSRC) has managed the redevelopment process and has overseen the refurbishing of many of Downtown Kingston's old buildings and also spearheaded a move to revitalize communities in the area.

Major efforts have been made in the last decade or so to revitalize the downtown area, particularly along the waterfront. Sited on the world's seventh largest natural harbor, and at the crossroads of the busy shipping lanes, the first move was to build a modern, computerized port facility, Port Bustamante to the west of the harbour outdated docks.

At the turn of the 21st century, there were talks of a Business Improvement District, in the Downtown Kingston area. In 2008, the new administration renewed this drive to revitalise and rejuvenate Downtown Kingston. The Urban Development Corporation and other private companies have all come on board to restore the Kingston Market District, a waterfront Festival Market, a Multi-Modal Transportation Hub (completed), a Kingston Harbour Bridge (linking Kingston, Norman Manley Airport and Historic Port Royal), a Railway Museum and Trade Centre, City Centre Park, a Justice Square, a new Parliament Building and the relocation of the Ministry of Foreign Affairs and Foreign Trade to downtown. Kingston is buzzing with excitement as construction work and road repairs are taking place all over. All of this is being done to encourage tourist and investors to the cultural hub of Downtown Kingston.

The new Digicel global headquarters, located on the waterfront, will be the most environmentally friendly major office building in the Caribbean using solar power, wind power and geothermal cooling systems. The relocation of the tele-communications giant to downtown, Kingston is a major boost for the ongoing revitalization of the area.

The Craft Market has also been relocated to the western end of the waterfront. A covered market, its small walkways of stalls and shops overflow with craftwork of excellent quality: straw goods, carving and articles in wood and local marble, jewelry, hand-made musical instruments, exquisite needlework and clothing as well as the usual souvenirs. It's the ideal place for the visitor to find something truly "Jamaican" to take home.

The National Gallery is home of Jamaica's premier art collection and is the cultural center of downtown Kingston. It houses several important works, mostly by artists from Jamaica, including Mallica "Kapo" Reynolds, Cecil Baugh, Albert Huie, Carl Abrahams and Edna

Jamaica Pegasus Hotel, New Kingston

Manley. The National Gallery also exhibits works by various international artists and traveling exhibitions and it offers research material on Jamaican art and culture.

A wonderful showcase also, for the talents of Jamaican fine artists, is the National Gallery, located on the waterfront in the Roy West Building. The Gallery is arranged to display recent works of established as well as new artists, and one section is devoted to works of the past including those with Jamaican connections.

On Kingston's eastern border, where mineral baths once revitalized old bodies, chimney stacks of a flour mill and a booming cement industry stand like sentinels against the skyline. Across the harbor lies the Norman Manley International Airport (NMIA), which is the primary airport for business travel to and from Jamaica and for the movement of cargo.

Kingston is a very modern, exciting city with a unique pulse that simply cannot be felt anywhere else in the world. The nightlife is great and the city is home to Fiction Lounge, Club Privilege and the Quad, all of which provide a premier clubbing experience. Dinning in the city is a great experience with a wide variety of restaurants and lounges to choose from. From the 'pan chicken' man on the side-walk who offer jerked chicken and pork, to the laid back vibe of Cuddyz Sport Bar, Susie's Bakery & Coffee Bar and Tracks & Records to the more formal settings of South Beach and Café Aubergine Bistro & Wine Bar, the city offers a vibrant range of menus to satisfy even the most discerning palate.

For accommodation, visitors have a wide variety of first class hotels to choose from such as Spanish Court Hotel and the Jamaica Pegasus.

Spanish Court Hotel, New Kingston

Tracks and Records, 'Market Place', Kingston

Kingston is home to the National Stadium, an impressive structure that is home to thousands of screaming fans whenever the Reggae Boyz (the national football team) play there, as well as the various athletic events such as the ISSA Boys and Girls Championships and the Jamaica National Invitational Meet which features several of the world's top athletes, most of whom are our very own such as Usain Bolt, Shelly-Ann Frazer-Pryce, Asafa Powell, Veronica Campbell- Brown and Yohan Blake.

In the background of Kingston looms the 7,402 foot Blue Mountain peak, looking on proudly at the melting pot of Jamaica's social, cultural, commercial and intellectual hub. Kingston, the proud sun-kissed Queen of Caribbean Cities.

Meanwhile, private developers have covered the old Liguanea cow pastures – and the hills beyond – with thousands of new homes. On the mountain slopes, storied mansions tell of the general prosperity generated below. Plain Tom Brown is neighbour to the Hon. Sir John Brown, and neither objects. This is a social democracy, Jamaican style.

Expressing the limitless freedom and equality guaranteed all Jamaicans by the Constitution, Kingstonians still keep reaching out for more of the good things, never quite content with each new gain; never stopping at each new stop; fiercely, and often vociferously, proud that theirs is the capital of Jamaica – sun-kissed Queen of Caribbean Cities.

Spanish Court Hotel, New Kingston

FRONTLINERS

A country's progress, its thrust into the future, is blue printed, engineered and managed by its leading citizens. The most dynamic, courageous, resourceful and resilient, sooner or later, forge to the frontline of doers and achievers.

They broaden existing fields and pioneer new ones. They introduce or develop new technology for doing things faster and better, as well as for doing new things. They anticipate, they initiate and they innovate. They see opportunities where others see obstacles.

In taking big gambles that do not always pay off, they transform raw landspace into beautiful new townships. They push back forests and sea and move mountains to create new landscapes. They partner with government in areas where government needs partners.

They carry mental and physical workloads, which make other men shiver and sweat just to contemplate. They dream where lesser mortals merely sleep. Staggering bank overdrafts do not faze them. Some build and lose several fortunes in their lifetime.

They are a breed who buck the odds – and conquer while etching their names on the foundation stones of national development. Some even become millionaires.

Jamaica is rich in this breed; first generation offspring emerging from obscurity; second or third generation whose grandparents came as indentured laborers from China and India, or as penniless peddlers from the Middle East; blacks whose ancestors came from Africa in slave ships.

Though their racial background are as varied as the fields in which they shine, they share a common heritage of being born and bred on an island where opportunity abounds and challenges beckon the enterprising; where every citizen, regardless of race or color, is free to

KAY N. OSBORNE

During her tenure as General Manager of Television Jamaica (TVJ), she led teams that developed TVJ's new business model and transformation processes with outstanding results, including achieving unprecedented audience share and revenue growth. Prior to joining TVJ, she served in executive positions with Fortune 500 companies and emerging growth companies in the United States, leading strategic initiatives in more than forty countries worldwide. In addition to her corporate role, she is a playwright and fine artist. Her plays have been performed in major cities in the UK and North America, and her paintings have been exhibited at Chicago's Museum of Science and Industry. Her resignation from TVJ took effect February 2012.

IAN G. WILKINSON

An attorney-at-law by profession, he runs his own law firm in Kingston and has taught law (Succession/Probate Practice and Procedure and Advocacy) at the Norman Manley Law School for the past twenty-one years. He has served in various capacities on the Bar Council of the Jamaican Bar Association and since 2011, he has sat on the Rules Committee of the Supreme Court and the Court of Appeal. In 2006, he was elected by the world chess governing body to serve as a judge on the World Chess Court, being the first person from the English-speaking Caribbean to have this honour.

DONNA DUNCAN-SCOTT

In 1998, she took on the mantle of Managing Director of Jamaica Money Market Brokers (JMMB) and during her tenure, she maintained the company's premier position as leader of the industry and together with the team, established the largest brokerage house in the Caribbean. She has received several awards on behalf of the company, as well as on her own merit, most notably the Jamaica Chamber of Commerce 'Best of Chamber' award for 2000 and the 'Business Leader of the Year' award for 2001 from the Jamaica Observer. She is currently Group Executive Director with responsibilities for Culture and Leadership Development.

GASSAN AZAN

He is the Chairman and Chief Executive Officer of MegaMart Wholesale Club which has been in operation since 2000 and has three branches (Kingston, Portmore and Montego Bay) with a fourth branch to be constructed in Mandeville. He is also Chief Executive Officer of Bashco, a chain of low-end stores that specializes in household goods, appliances, furniture and clothing targeted at consumers in the low-income bracket. Committed to the development of downtown Kingston, he opened the multimillion dollar Sweet Tings Bakery in late 2010.

KENNETH "KENNY" BENJAMIN

He is the Founder and Executive Chairman of Guardsman Group Limited. The first company, Guardsman Limited, was founded in 1977 and is Jamaica's largest security conglomerate. He went on to establish Guardsman Armoured, Guardsman Alarms, Guardsman Elite, Guardsman Communications, Guardsman Training Centre and Marksman Limited, a stand-alone security brand. In 2004 he received the Jamaica Observer 'Business Leader of the Year' award and in 2005 he was the recipient of the prestigious Paul Harris Pin by the Rotary Club of Kingston in recognition of his philanthropic contributions.

reach out in any area of enterprise he chooses – free to become a frontliner if he has what it takes, or make a mess trying.

The seventies saw the flight of thousands of these erstwhile frontliners due to the then government's policy of Democratic Socialism which was seen as the death knell of free enterprise, despite assurances to the contrary. The loss was more than the estimated $450 million in capital that they took at a time when the economy was beginning to wobble (partly as a result of external factors beyond Jamaicas control). The greater loss was in the quality of brainpower that made each migrant a frontliner in his field, a vital cog in the economic machine.

Democratic Socialism created a new crop of frontliners. Whereas the old crop was of men and women who produced wealth and new institutions which every country needs, the new crop was largley of people who administered what was created by others – a crop of super bureaucrats, a new elite hitherto unknown in Jamaica. Socialism aimed at distributing the wealth, which capitalism and free enterprise combined to produce. The super bureaucrat presides over the process of distributing such wealth while it lasts.

With the change in government and a stabilized economy, many of the old frontliners began to return, swelling the ranks of those who had remained. In the interim, another generation of frontliners was born of adversity, as vigorously committed to the free enterprise system as ever. Some of the new breed are excellent men and women. As private entrepreneurs, they have emerged on the front line of success in whatever fields they entered.

As we move forward to another fifty years of growth and prosperity for our beloved nation, we present those who, through their hard work, vision and relentless drive, are helping this little dot on the map to achieve greatness in so many different areas.

CHRISTOPHER RICHARD ISSA, JP

He is an attorney-at-law, hotelier, philanthropist, real estate developer and publisher. He is the head of the Chrissa Group which acquired the former Spanish Court Shopping Center and transformed it into a spacious 107-room, contemporary-style urban hotel with a Sky Terrace highlighted by a 50-foot, mosaic tiled infinity edge lap pool.

PATRICE WILSON-MCHUGH

She is Jamaica's first Master Mixologist and the Managing Director of Jamaica's leading beverage and catering entity, the Bars To Go Group of Companies, home to seven subsidiaries including Bars To Go Party Services Ltd., Gourmet To Go Catering Services Ltd. and Bars To Go Training Institute which certifies students to practice bartending, mixology, food & beverage and commercial food preparation anywhere in the CARICOM region. She has been featured in the Wall Street Journal for her contribution to the field of mixology and she is the founder and president of the Jamaica Bartending Guild.

LASCELLES AUGUSTA CHIN, OJ, CD

The founder and executive chairman of the LASCO Affiliated Companies, he is one of Jamaica's most distinguished and respected entrepreneurs, a pioneering exporter, outstanding philanthropist, and a much honoured leader in Jamaica and the Caribbean. In October 2010, LASCO became the first company in the history of Jamaica that had three affiliated companies listed at the same time on the Jamaica Stock Exchange. He is a dynamic chairman of several state agencies and has served as Director for in excess of 15 companies.

WAYNE CHEN

He is the Chief Executive Officer of Super Plus Food Stores, Jamaica's largest retailer, and he is also the Chairman of NCB Insurance Limited and West Indies Trust Company Limited. The recipient of many awards, he was the Jamaica Junior Chamber 1994 Outstanding Young Person of Jamaica (for Outstanding Entrepreneurial Accomplishment), the Jamaica Observer 1998 Business Leader of the Year, and in 2006, he was an Inductee of the Manchester Hall of Fame and the Jamaica Institute of Management Fellow of the Institute.

ABRAHAM A. MANDARA Ph.D.

An educator at Wolmer's Preparatory School for twenty-one years before his retirement in 2011, he held the positions of Supervisor of the Upper School, Supervisor of the school's resource centre, and was also Vice Principal during his last six years there. For the past ten years he has authored fourteen primary education text-books and edited many others. He is a reader of various subject manuscripts for international publishers and is also a business administration consultant and motivational speaker. He does a lot of community service, especially in seriously depressed areas.

JEROME O. HAMILTON

Founder of Headline Entertainment, the largest booking firm in the Caribbean responsible for the public relations and booking engagements of artistes such as Sean Paul, Damian Marley, Stephen Marley and Barrington Levy to name a few. He has been a prominent name in the forefront of Jamaican and Caribbean entertainment since the 1990s. Highly regarded for his knowledge of the music industry, he has been called upon to consult on major music festivals and events including the 2007 Cricket World Cup opening ceremony; the Jamaica Jazz & Blues Festival; Reggae Sumfest; The St. Kitts Music Festival and the Turks & Caicos Music and Culture Festival.

AUDREY P. MARKS MBA, B.Sc

Jamaica's 10th and first female Ambassador to the United States, and Permanent Representative to the Organization of American States, she is the founder of Paymaster (Jamaica) Limited, a multi-transaction company which she conceptualized and started in 1997. Paymaster operates payment agencies from which all types of bill payments and application services can be made. In its 15th year, Paymaster has created 150 agencies in Jamaica and the USA, providing services to over 1.4M customers and employment for over 400 persons with annual transactions of up to $60 Billion Dollars. It is the first multi-transaction agency in the Caribbean.

DON WEHBY

He is group Chief Executive Officer at Grace Kennedy Limited and a former Senator and cabinet minister. In September 2007, he became a Senator and Minister Without Portfolio in the Ministry of Finance and The Public Service. He returned to Grace Kennedy Limited in 2009 and became the company's group Chief Operating Officer. He is Chairman of the Taskforce on Tourism Contribution & Linkages and is also Vice President of the Private Sector Organization of Jamaica (PSOJ). He previously served the PSOJ as a member of its Economic Policy Committee and Honorary Treasurer.

HON. GORDON BUTCH STEWART, OD, OJ

One of Jamaica's most influential and inspirational business leaders, he presides over a billion dollar business empire that has shaped the economic landscape of the Caribbean. Founder, Chairman & CEO of Appliance Traders Group of Companies (ATL), which includes Sandals Resorts, one of the world's biggest brands, his business interests incorporate over twenty separate companies that are collectively Jamaica's largest private sector group, the country's biggest foreign exchange earner and its largest non-government employer.

RICHARD BYLES B.Sc, MSc

He has been the President and Chief Executive Officer of Sagicor Life Jamaica Ltd., a subsidiary of Sagicor Financial Corp., since March 2004. Prior to that, he served as the President and Chief Executive Officer of Pan Jamaican Investment Trust Limited (Pan Jam), from 1991 to February 2004, where he chaired the trading, banking and insurance subsidiaries; pursuing a strategy of mergers, acquisition and divestments. He served as Vice President of the Private Sector Organization of Jamaica and represents them on the country's development council. He also serves as the Chairman of Red Stripe, the National Water Commission and Harmonization Limited, a Resort Development Company, owned by the Government of Jamaica.

HON. OLIVER CLARKE, OJ, Hon. LL.D, JP FCA

Former Chairman and Managing Director of The Gleaner Co. Ltd, his illustrious career includes stints as Chairman of the Jamaica National Building Society (JNBS), Chairman of National Commercial Bank (Jamaica) Ltd. and Chairman of Sangster's Book Stores Ltd. In 2004 he was recognized as a Caribbean Luminary by the American Foundation for the University of the West Indies and in 2009 he was conferred with the Honorary Doctor of Laws degrees from the University of the West Indies and the University of Technology, Jamaica.

MICHAEL LEE CHIN

He is an investor, bank owner and philanthropist. Founder and Chairman of Portland Holdings Inc., he has been profiled by Forbes magazine as one of the world's richest people. His net worth was at one time estimated to be 2.5 billion US dollars. Michael Lee-Chin's business accomplishments span various countries and numerous sectors. In 2002, Portland Holdings acquired the National Commercial Bank (NCB) Jamaica Ltd. and its subsidiaries. Since becoming part of the Portland group, NCB profits have increased to approximately US$100 million annually from US$6 million. NCB today stands as Jamaica's largest bank with 45 branches and 2,400 employees.

HORACE BURRELL

Former Captain in the Jamaica Defence Force (JDF), he is the President of The Jamaica Football Federation and oversaw Jamaica's historic qualification for the 1998 World Cup. He is also the co-owner of The Captain's Bakery Ltd., a bakery and grill chain with six locations island-wide and a branch in the Cayman Islands. The chain is a major sponsor of various football and cricket leagues across the island. He is also the owner of Captain's Aviation Services Ltd., a helicopter training school and commercial airlift service.

KINGSLEY COOPER, CD

An attorney-at-law, he is the Chairman of Pulse Investments Ltd., Chairman of Jamaica's Entertainment Advisory Board and Chairman of the Caribbean Fashion Industry Association. He founded Pulse Modelling Agency in 1980 and pioneered, defined and developed an international modeling industry for the Caribbean, in the process discovering and developing super-models and other international stars. At different periods, Pulse models have distinguished themselves as being among the best in the world. In 2005, he was awarded a star on the Reggae Red Carpet Walk of Fame, New York City, for his work in the development of the Caribbean's entertainment industry.

DR. HENRY LOWE, CD, JP, FRSH, ARIC

He is a scientist who specializes in medicinal chemistry and has contributed over 40 years in the fields of science and technology, energy, the environment, wellness and health sciences nationally, regionally and internationally. He is the Founder/Executive Chairman of the Environmental Health Foundation, Owner of Eden Gardens Wellness & Lifestyle Centre and also the Founder/Chairman of Bio-Tech R&D Institute Ltd., Jamaica. Dr. Lowe is the holder of a USA Patent for his anti-cancer discovery and he has co-authored numerous publications related to science, education, environment and health.

WILLIAM MAHFOOD

He is the managing director of the English-Speaking Caribbean's largest food and beverage distribution and manufacturing company, the Wisynco Group Ltd. He led Wisynco's diversification from being a producer of plastic, rubber and synthetic products to successfully produce Jamaica's most popular water brand – WATA. This success was extended into producing an award-winning flavoured water brand – Ocean Spray WATA. The Wisynco Group Ltd is also the proud producer of the BIGGA brand of carbonated beverages, while boasting Jamaica's first and only locally produced energy drink, BOOM. He launched Wisynco Foods – which operates three Wendy's locations, 11 Domino's Pizzas, and a Haagen Daaz bistro in Kingston.

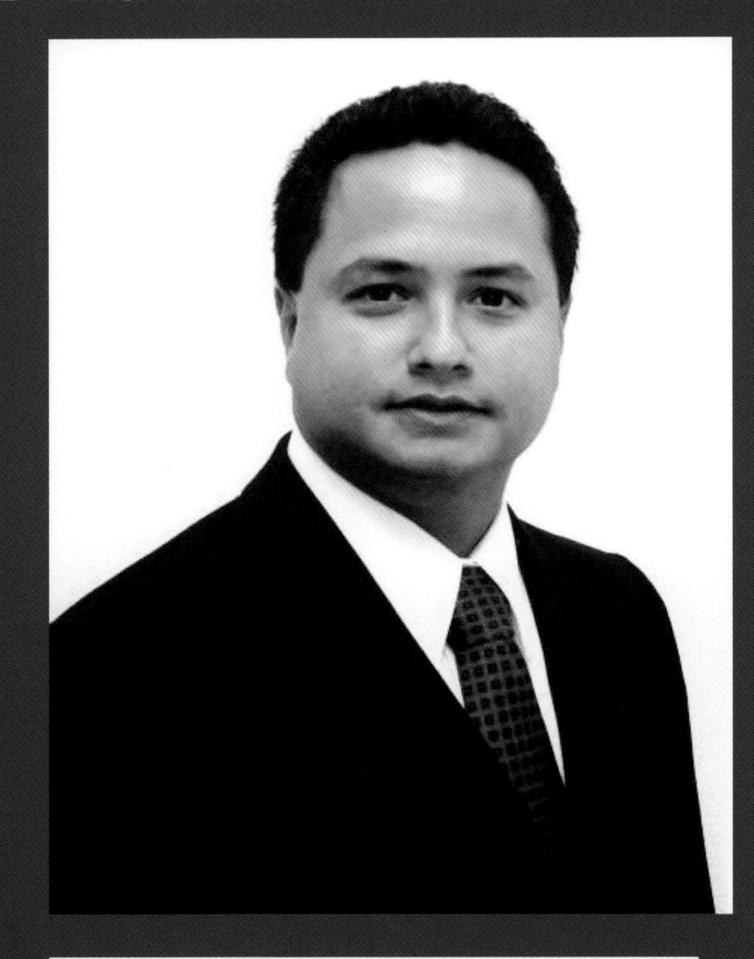

OMAR AZAN

He is the Chairman and Chief Executive Officer of Boss Furniture, and the immediate past president of the Jamaica Manufacturers' Association (JMA). An entrepreneur for over 15 years, he also serves on the Board of the Export-Import (EXIM) Bank of Jamaica, as the Budget Chair, on the Board of the Bureau of Standards Jamaica (BSJ) as Chairman and as a Board Member of the Jamaica Business Development Corporation (JBDC). He is widely respected among the local business community and his opinions and recommendations on economic and financial issues are widely sought after. He stands as a standard bearer for local manufacturing and sells the message 'buy Jamaican, build Jamaica' every opportunity he gets.

NOEL A. HYLTON, O.J., HON. LLD, C.D., J.P.

An accountant by profession, he has had considerable experience in both public and private sectors for more than 40 years. He is Chairman and also President & Chief Executive Officer of The Port Authority of Jamaica, and has had more than 40 years' experience in the Jamaican Shipping Industry. In 2001, the University of the West Indies conferred on Mr. Hylton, the Honorary Degree of Doctor of Laws (Hon. LLD), in recognition of his contribution to the region's maritime and shipping development. In January, 2004, Mr. Hylton received the "Gleaner Honour Award in the Category of Business for 2003", for his "superb work in transforming the nation's ports and for outstanding leadership qualities."

JOSEPH M. MATALON, B.SC. (HONS.) ECON.

He is the Chairman of ICD Group Limited, and Chairman of a number of ICD Group company boards, including CGM Gallagher Group Limited and British Caribbean Insurance Company Limited. Since 2007, he has also served as Chairman of the Development Bank of Jamaica, the Government of Jamaica's principal development finance institution. He was elected President of The Private Sector Organisation of Jamaica (PSOJ) in 2009 and in August 2010, he was awarded The Order of Distinction in the Rank of Commander for his contribution to the Private & Public Sectors and Community Service.

GLEN MILLS

Founder and President of the Racers Track Club, he is one of the most acclaimed sprint coaches in the world. He is the coach of the fastest sprinter the world has ever seen, Usain Bolt, the world record holder and Olympic record holder of both the men's 100 meters and 200 meters. Other world class sprinters that he has coached or is coaching include Kim Collins (gold medalist 100 meters 2003 World Championships), Warren Weir (bronze medalist 200 meters 2012 London Olympics) and Yohan Blake (gold medalist 100 meters 2011 World Championships, silver medalist 100 meters & 200 meters 2012 London Olympics). Racers Track Club trains at the University of the West Indies Mona.

Victoria Jubilee Children's Hosptial

Bellevue Hospital (Mental Institution)

Entrance to the Bustamante Hospital for Children

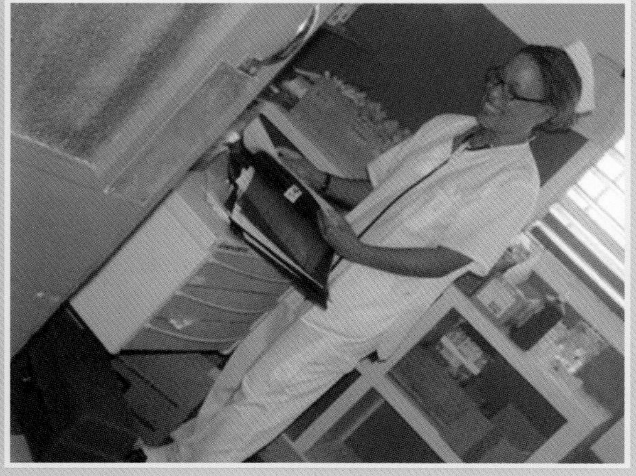

A nurse on duty

HEALTH

Education, health and agriculture, are Jamaica's parallel top priorities. Irrespective of which political party is in power; these are the areas on which the accent is heaviest. Each succeeding Prime Minister gives the same instruction to his Minister of Health: "Whatever else you do, keep the nation healthy, for therein lies our strength to survive economic hardship".

In the field of medical expertise, what Jamaica lacks in quantity is made up for in quality. Thanks to the excellent contacts maintained with other countries, also to the World Health Organization (WHO), Jamaica has quick access to scientific modern health resources, which may be lacking at home when some new threat to the nation's health is discovered.

In none of the national services is there greater dedication than in health. There is no let-up in monitoring the environment to keep it safe for Jamaicans and the thousands of visitors who give meaning to the tourist trade.

Nobody is happy about the thin spread of medical and technical back-up personnel. To prevent it from becoming even thinner, the government has, over the years, undertaken extensive programmes in population control education. By press, radio, television, posters and on the platform, the population has been encouraged to practice birth control and have fewer childern. These programmes have also been extended to provide information and counselling about HIV/STD's and preventative methods to be used.

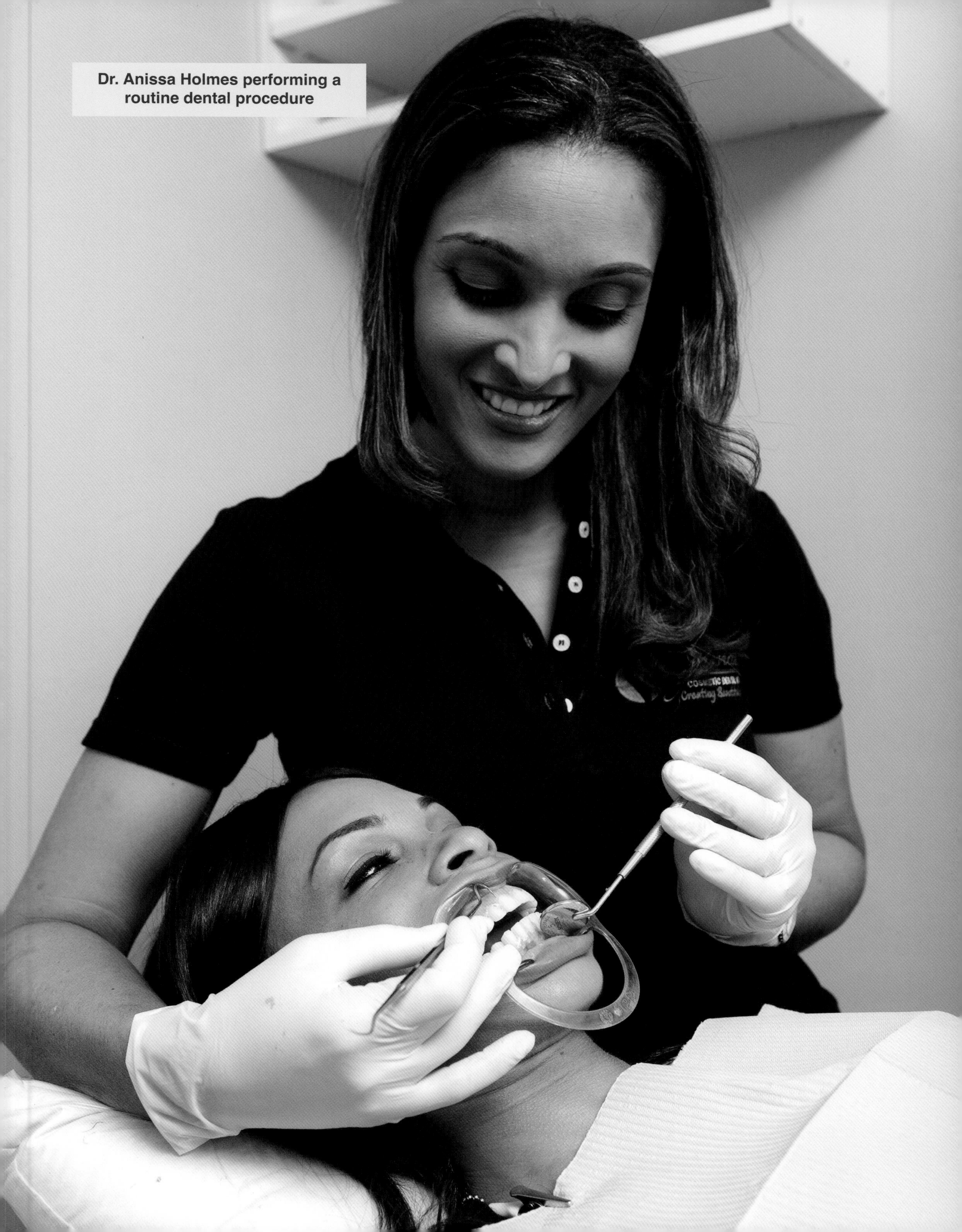

Dr. Anissa Holmes performing a routine dental procedure

In 2007, the government introduced free healthcare for children under the age of 18. By 2008, there was a comprehensive health plan that saw the abolition of user fees in all government hospitals and clinics, this also includes prescription drugs. There are 29 public hospitals in the island. Of these 18 are general (at least 1 in each parish), 5 are poly-clinics, and 6 are specialist hospitals.

The oldest house of healing is the Kingston Public Hospital on North Street, in the teeming heart of the capital. It was first established by English Governor, Sir John Peter Grant, in 1869, as a hospital for sailors and sited on West Street. The newest is the May Pen Hospital in Clarendon, which was built to replace the former structure and reopened late in 1977.

There is also the expansive teaching hospital of the University of the West Indies at Mona, in Kingston, with its Faculty of Medical Sciences.

Private hospitals have long been part of the Jamaican Health scene. Major ones in Kingston are St. Joseph's, Nuttall, Andrews Memorial and Medical Associates.

In addition to hospitals, a number of services keep continuous watch over essential areas of the nation's health.

These include the Public Health Department, the Bureau of Health Education, Insect Vector Control, dental care, child feeding programs, radiography and radiotherapy services, and the Hyacinth Lightbourne (Visiting) Nursing Service.

Primary health care is carried out mainly through 361 health centres across the island. There are also 34 special clinics of which 10 are dedicated to family planning, and 24 are school dental clinics (6 being mobile facilities).

Kingston Public Hospital, an over 200 year old medical institution.

Spanish Town Hospital

Top: Nuttall Memorial Hospital sign
Bottom: Medical Associates Hospital

INDUSTRY

In his moment of elation, Columbus named it Santo Gloria, but the aboriginal Taino Indians who welcomed his landing party, had already named it Xaymaca, meaning "Land of Wood and Water". The English, who came 150 years later, simply called it Jamaica, and marveled at its beautiful mountains and fertile land.

Jamaica is favored with a resource base which provides significant scope for ecomonic growth, its total area is approximately 2.7 million acres. It has 1.68 million acres in farms and these are suitable for many forms of agriculture, including forestry.

The land produces the food Jamaicans eat most and the crops they export (to pay for the things they import). This includes sugar, bananas, citrus, coffee, cocoa, pimento, ginger, fruit – both fresh and canned and flowers.

Farm land accounts for nearly 334,000 acres. Some 209,000 of these comprise farms from four to ten acres each. This acreage is responsible for the yams, breadfruit, corn, potatoes, beans, peas, cocoa, avocado, green vegetables, pineapples, pawpaw (papaya) and plantains.

Jamaicans think of their major products in terms of gold. Sugar is brown gold; bananas, once bigger than sugar but now a poor second, is green gold; bauxite is red gold (though the bauzite industry has seen a downward trend in recent years); citrus (oranges, grapefruits, ortaniques, tangerine) is sun-gold – they look golden in the sun when ripe.

The island also produces fine herds of beef and dairy cattle: Santa Gertrudis, Holstein, Jamaica Hope

(developed by Jamaican scientist Dr. Thomas P. Lecky), Aberdeen Angus, Zebu, Brahaman – evidence of the long, patient, scientific build up from the wild herds left behind by the Spanish, and pedigree breeding stock imported since the early 1920s. The Jamaican Hope breed is a potential winner by popular acclaim. The finest herd is the Santa Gretrudis, developed by Reynolds Jamaica Mines in their lush Lydford pastures, as a part of the agricultural thrust of their vast operation.

Every year, in the first week of August, the pride of these herds is paraded at Denbigh, the Jamaica Agricultural Society's showground at May Pen in Clarendon. They are viewed by 20-50,000 showgoers and judged by men and women knowledgeable in cattle and small livestock. Many prize bulls and heifers are often sold on the spot to Latin American cattlemen who make Denbigh an annual must, thus giving Jamaica a prestigious, though modest, cattle export trade.

Sugar and tobacco are legacies of the Spaniards, but it was the English who turned sugar into brown gold and established the plantation system. It was an American – Captain L.D. Baker of Boston, Massachusetts – who, long after emancipation, started sugar's first great decline, and turned the banana into green gold.

Jamaica's Blue Mountain coffee needs no introduction to connoisseurs or lovers of fine coffee anywhere. This product has, in the last decade or so, attracted a new breed of gentle-man farmer for whom quality control is of supreme concern. As an export product, its value to the Jamaican economy cannot be over emphasised, being the second largest traded commodity in the world.

Jamaica's fisheries are comprised of marine, fresh water and inland fish farming.

Marine fishing is done mainly by fishermen operating from canoes, with the Morant and Pedro banks being the two largest offshore fishing areas.

Inland fisheries have been recording significant growth in recent years, and have enhanced the population's protein intake.

Jamaica's non-traditonal export crops are being given increased attention for development. These include winter vegetables, tubers, ornamental (horticulture), pumpkins and mangoes for northern markets. Ornamental exports have shown sustained growth trends, which can be linked to marketing strategies being employed by the various export marketing agencies, as well as initiatives taken by growers themselves.

The Ministry of Agriculture has been championing for us to "Grow what we eat... Eat what we grow." The government believes that we should eat as much as we grow to reduce the importation of the same goods that we produce. The Ministry has also hosted a number of farmers' markets across the island.

How to make the land produce more with fewer hands is the problem which government, private planners and investors, jointly, must solve in order to achieve progressively better profit levels in agriculture, and higher living standards for all Jamaicans.

Jamaica's music industry is a major earner of foreign exchange and provider of creative employment opportunities for a large number and diverse group of Jamaicans. Music is one of Jamaica's most successful exports, with artistes like the late great Bob Marley, bands like Third World, and dancehall aces Shabba Ranks and Sean Paul selling millions of albums worldwide, and influencing countless reggae and dancehall acts across the globe. The music industry continues to boost sectors such as

MAERSK
POLICE
WHALER
YAMAHA

tourism, with annual music festivals and shows such as Reggae Sumfest, Appleton Temptation Isle Weekend and Rebel Salute bringing in thousands of visitors from around the world.

As the industry continues to grow and evolve, there is need for increased investment in areas such as the introduction and upgrading of the production and distribution technology, studio construction,

sponsorship of events and business support services.

The government has introduced incentives such as duty free importation of musicians' tools of trade to aid in the development of the industry. Local corporations have in recent times created successful advertising campaigns with dancehall music and culture as the central theme.

JAMAICA: PLACE TO INVEST

Norman Manley International Airport

Jamaica Stock Exchange, Kingston

Highway under construction, St. Catherine

Red Stripe Brewery, Kingston

Successive Governments in Jamaica have recognized that private investments have a vital role to play in the development of Jamaica.

Jamaica offers opportunities for a wide range of investments and these are being vigorously exploited through joint ventures between local and overseas private sector entrepreneurs, in the production and marketing of goods for the domestic and overseas markets.

As part of the programme to encourage investments in Jamaica, the Jamaica National Investment Programme Limited (JNIP), was established in 1981 as the executing agency for government's investment promotion efforts as was the Jamaica National Export Corporation (JNEC), both of which have been merged into one organization known as JAMPRO. JAMPRO's primary purpose is to stimulate investments and facilitate efficient and speedy response to inquiries made by local and foreign investors, and to centralize under one roof, the processing of investment proposals relating to all sectors of the economy. Since 1980, there has been a phenomenal growth in new investments in Jamaica, auguring well for continued development.

Strategic Location: The island is strategically located geographically, being on the centre of the shipping routes from North America and Europe, to the Panama Canal, South America and the Far East. Over thirty international shipping lines call regularly, providing oceanic and regional feeder services to two international seaports, one in Kingston on the south coast, the seventh largest natural harbour in the world, and the other in Montego Bay on the north coast.

Bank of Jamaica

At the port in Kingston, there are lift-on, lift-off and roll-on, roll-off facilities for handling container cargo. There are also facilities for handling break-bulk cargo, with the same facilities available at Montego Bay. By ocean, Jamaica is only two to five days from the Panama Canal and about eleven days from the Pacific ports.

Jamaica has three international airports, one in the capital, Kingston, the other in Montego Bay, and the smallest in Boscobel, St. Mary all three are served by a growing number of international airlines. Flying time from Kingston to New York is 3 1/2 hours.

Infrastructure: Public utilities have undergone extensive expansion in recent years. Electricity generating capacity is continuously being upgraded to keep pace with demand and there is an on going programme of refurbishing equipment; alternate energy sources are being developed which will considerably reduce dependency on oil for energy (except automotive fuel) during the next decade.

Data indicates that Jamaica ranks high among other developing countries in terms of road miles per unit area. In fact, Jamaica has the second highest number of miles per capita, second only to Japan. Its multi-million dollar port in Kingston provides the Caribbean's premier transshipment facility. Adjacent to the port is a Free Zone complex, with another in Montego Bay, which provides access to world markets.

With an impressive modern communications system including 2G, 3G and 4G mobile coverage, uploading videos, browsing the internet and streaming music at an amazing speed have never been easier.

Islandwide internet, mobile, and landline coverage, including facsimile, ensure efficient communication with the rest of the world.

Wigton Wind Farm, St, Elizabeth

Jamaica has a well-developed financial system embracing a range of institutions. These include a Central Bank, a Development Bank, Mortgage Bank, several commercial banks (some affiliates of international banks), a number of merchant banks, a Stock Exchange, and a Unit Trust Scheme. There are trust companies, a wide range of insurance companies, and building societies. All major towns are served by one or more of these institutions.

Statistical data in the following areas, among others, are published monthly, quarterly or annually by the Department of Statistics: National Income, Monetary Statistics, Labour Force, External Trade, Production, Consumer Prices, Demography, Employment and Wages in large establishments. An annual Economic and Social survey is prepared by the Planning Institute of Jamaica. In fact, there is hardly a major area of activity for which regular and accurate statistics are not available on request, and for little or no charge.

Health: Jamaica rates among the healthiest countries of the world, having achieved a high degree of success in its conquest of killer diseases commom to the tropics, and many of those "imported" from sub-tropical and temperate countries.

Its medical services are staffed by competent personnel. Community health centres, private and public hospitals, pharmacies and teaching hospitals with international accreditation, combine to provide a continuing health programme of high quality. Health facilities are available to non-Jamaicans on the same terms and conditions as to the indigenous population. In few words, Jamaica is one of the healthiest and most wholesome places on earth in which to live and work.

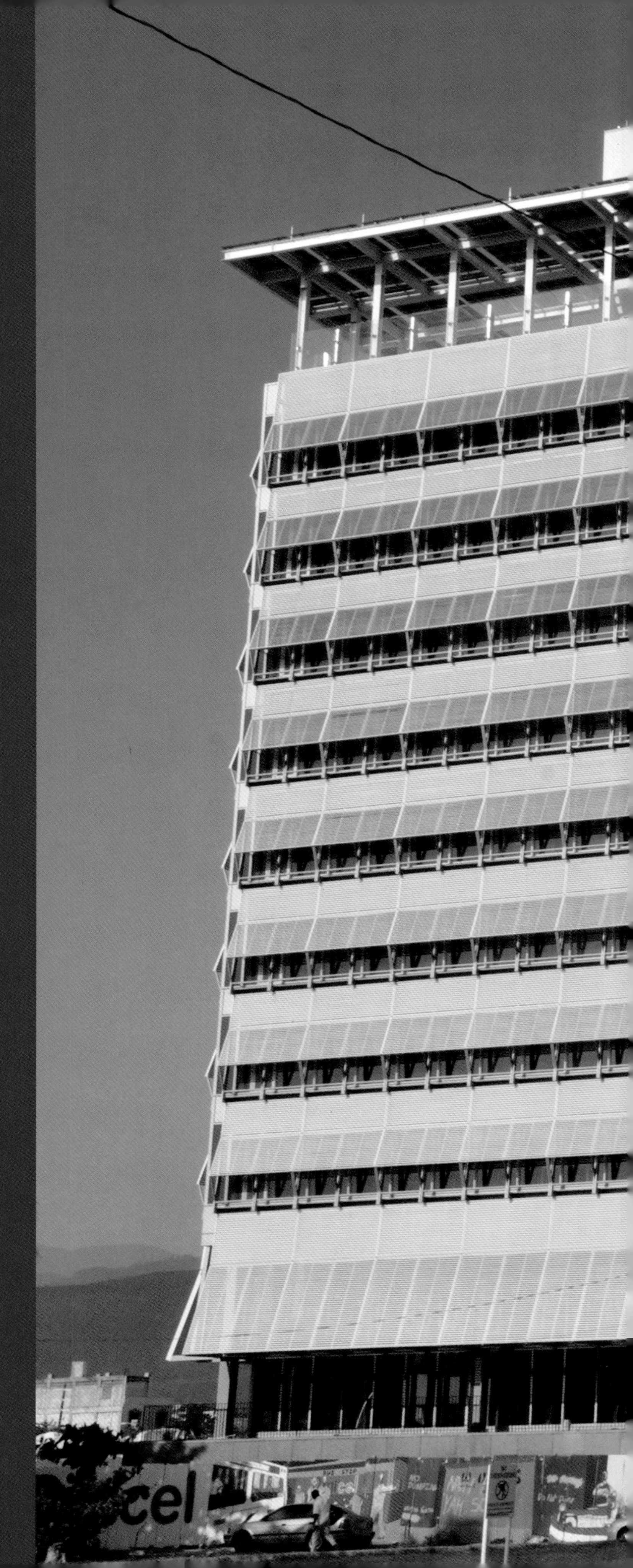

The new Digicel Corporate Headquarters, Downtown, Kingston

Corporate Headquarters of National Commercial Bank, New Kingston

Present needs are for additional medical personnel to replace those who have migrated and to staff rural clinics. Health facilities in the rural areas are constantly being upgraded, and a recruitment drive for medical personnel has been most successful.

Labour Force: Jamaica has the largest English-speaking labour force in the Caribbean. The labour pool has demonstrated an ability to respond quickly to training and adapt to modern technology. Various training programmes exist, within industries providing skills training and upgrading, supervisory skills and leadership skills training. A number of institutions, including JAMPRO are available to assist companies in these efforts.

Through the principle of collective bargaining, workers are free to join trade unions of their choice. Among the major trade unions in Jamaica are the Bustamante Industrial Trade Union (BITU) and the National Workers Union (NWU). There is also an employers group, the Jamaica Employers' Federation (JEF) which provides timely advice for its members whenever problems arise (e.g. contract preparation, negotiation and administration).

Market Access: Jamaica has vast opportunities to acces the markets of the U.S.A., Canada, Europe and the Caribbean, as a beneficiary of various trade agreements with these regions. Jamaica currently offers a package of preferential trade agreements unsurpassed by any other country in the world, assisted by the USA'S passage of the Caribbean Basin Initiative (CBI) and the Canada/Caribbean Trade Agreement (CARIBCAN), both pioneered by Edward Seaga. Jamaica has seen significant growth in non-traditional exports to the USA, with the garment industry leading the way.

The Jamaican Advantage: Perhaps the greatest need of any company today is that of information and the transfer of data. Realizing this, the Seaga government introduced Jamaica Digiport International Ltd., (JDI Ltd.) so that companies who wish to seize the Jamaican advantage can receive high quality switched data services, toll-free calling and international long distacne service. JDI Ltd.'s services are designed to meet the exacting standards of AT&T, 5ESS switch and the AT&T Integrated Access Terminal (IAT) located in the Montego Bay Free Zone. JDI Ltd. forms part of a complex of information processing and electronic assembly companies.

All these services are further supported by private local companies which provide up-to-date data and information training, as well as management. One such leading company is the Achievement Centre Ltd., located in Kingston with a representative in Montego Bay.

Foreign Investment Policy: Jamaica has a long record of partnership with foreign investors in the developmennt of a wide range of products and highly productive industries. These industries include, first and foremost, bauxite/alumina, currently the second largest source in the world involving the participation of North America's five largest aluminium corporations. There are currently over 200 foreign companies or subsidiaries operating in the island.

It must be noted with much pride that since independence, there have been no instance of a foreign-based company, or a Jamaican company with foreign partnership closing down its operations and leaving the island on account of difficulties with any government regime. Whichever of the two leading political parties is in office, each individually goes to

New Falmouth Pier; a new era in cruise shipping

great pains to give the foreign investors fullest possible protection. Jamaica realizes its need of foreign investment to develop its resources and provide a better life for its population.

Warren Weir, Usain Bolt, Yohan Blake

Flag formation at the Jamaica 50 Grand Gala

Friends enjoying the Jamaica 50 Celebrations

Heritage House, Duke Street, Kingston

JAMAICA 50 & BEYOND

The year 2012 was a significant one for Jamaica and all Jamaicans. It marked our 50th year of independence as a nation and Jamaicans at home and abroad celebrated with unbridled joy and pride, dressed in their black, green and gold in various styles. Flags were patriotically displayed on vehicles, light poles, buildings and homes.

Jamaica, in those fifty years, has grown by leaps and bounds in many areas, and brand Jamaica today, is one of the strongest brands in the world. The island has excelled in areas such as the arts, sports and academics, impacting the world in unprecedented and unparalleled fashion for a nation of its size.

The celebrations began in January 2012 with Jamaica 50th themed New Year's balls and fireworks on the waterfront in downtown Kingston. The Archbishop of York, the Most Reverend and Rt. Honourable Dr. John Sentamu, visited Jamaica from January 21-31 and hosted two Ecumenical Services to celebrate Jamaica 50. Official celebrations continued in June with the National Senior Athletic Championships at the National Stadium and the Jamaica Military Tattoo at Up Park Camp, a breathtaking and elaborate display of marching bands, precision drill movements and dynamic military displays, as well as performances by other organizations and agencies.

Top: Emancipation Park decorated in celebration of Jamaica 50
Bottom: The entrance to Jamaica House

The 2012 London Olympics was next, and our athletes, Usain Bolt in particular, were the toast of the games. Alia Atkinson got the ball rolling with her captivating swimming, making the final of the women's 100m breast stroke where she placed fourth, just missing out on the bronze medal. Samantha Albert, Jamaica's lone equestrienne, also did Jamaica proud in her event. Shelly-Ann Fraser-Pryce successfully defended her Olympic 100m title, becoming only the third woman in history to do so. She added two silver medals to her tally, placing second in the 200m and the 4x100m relays. Usain Bolt created history by becoming the first man ever to retain the sprint double by successfully defending his Olympic 100m and 200m crowns, setting a new Olympic record for the former. Jamaica received a wonderful independence gift when Bolt, Yohan Blake and newcomer Warren Weir went 1-2-3, claiming all three medals in the 200m. Jamaicans around the world swelled with pride as the national anthem played at the medal ceremony with three Jamaicans on the podium. The 4 x 100m relay team of Usain Bolt, Yohan Blake, Nesta Carter and Michael Frater closed out the games with a flourish, winning the gold and setting a new world record (36.84s), becoming the first relay team in history to go under 37 seconds. Kenneth Edwards, Jamaica's first ever qualifier at the Olympic Games in the Tae Kwon Do event, also represented his country well. Jamaica's medal tally at the end of the

The crowd at Half-Way-Tree, Kingston immediately following the 200m race at the 2012 London Olympics

Scenes from the Jamaica 50 Grand Gala

games was 12: 4 gold, 4 silver, 4 bronze. The Jamaican team made their nation proud and definitely added something special to the independence celebrations.

The Jamaica 50 Jubilee Village which ran from August 1-6 at Independence Park, had art and craft displays, food courts, children's village and live performances, entertaining thousands of Jamaicans by showcasing the island's rich and vibrant culture. The celebrations culminated in spectacular fashion on August 6 with the Jamaica 50 Grand Gala at the also 50 year old National Stadium (it was officially opened in 1962). The venue was a sea of black, green and gold as thousands of Jamaicans jubilantly celebrated, revelling in the delightful and colourful presentations, some of which paid tribute to our cultural icons in the performing arts. Several foreign dignitaries, including President of the Nation of Islam, the Hon. Minister Louis Farrakhan; former United States Secretary of State, Colin Powell; President of the Republic of South Africa, His Excellency Jacob Zuma, also shared in the celebration. The five-hour long Gala, dubbed 'Tributes in Gold', ended in a spectacular display of fireworks.

The Jamaica 50 mission was to deepen the spirit of patriotism and nationalism of Jamaicans at home and abroad and engage the world through a series of planned activities and projects which will rekindle a sense of pride in our independence as a nation and create a lasting legacy. By all accounts, the mission was accomplished.

A Tribute to Two Cultural Icons

There are many people who have made invaluable contributions to the development of this small but great nation, and here we highlight two, a son and a daughter that Lady Jamaica has produced.

THE HON. REX NETTLEFORD, OM, FIJ, OCC

Former Vice Chancellor of the University of the West Indies, Director of the Trade Union Education Institute, actor, dancer, author, sociologist, choreographer and director & founder of the National Dance Theatre Company (NDTC). He had the distinction of having been called upon by virtually every Government in the Caribbean throughout his career, and also acted as a consultant for numerous international organizations, including CARICOM, the Organization of American States, UNESCO, the International Labour Organization, the World Bank, and the International Development Research Council, of which he was a founding director.

Here, we will focus on his contributions to Jamaican culture through dance.

In 1962, Nettleford founded the National Dance Theatre Company of Jamaica (NDTC), an ensemble of dancers, musicians, technicians and designers, which focused on fusing together traditional Jamaican music, dance and rituals, and re-introducing them to the Jamaican populace. As the NDTC's artistic director and principal choreographer until his death in 2010, Nettleford artistically portrayed the indigenous practices of Kumina, Pocomania and the rich folk music traditions from across the island. This he believed would ensure the survival of Jamaica's culture and progression towards a national identity.

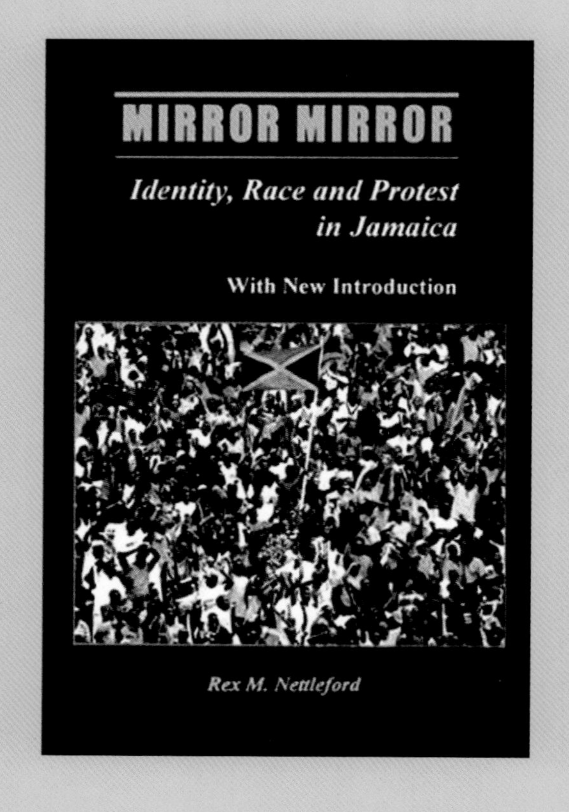

THE HON. LOUISE BENNETT-COVERLEY
O.M. O.J. M.B.E. DIP R.A.D.A., D. LITT (HON)

Affectionately known as "Miss Lou", she was a poet, folklorist, writer, and educator. Miss Lou wrote and performed her poems in patois, which was instrumental in having this "dialect" of the Jamaican people given literary recognition in its own right. She was recognized as Jamaica's leading comedienne and appeared in leading humorous roles in several Jamaican pantomimes and television shows. She travelled throughout the world promoting the culture of Jamaica through lectures and performances. She achieved international fame and was a celebrity at home in Jamaica, the United Kingdom and Canada, where she spent the last decade of her life. Her work has been published several times, most notably the volumes 'Jamaica Labrish' in 1966 and 'Anancy and Miss Lou' in 1979. She has done recordings as well and her most influential recording is probably her 1954 rendition of the Jamaican traditional song "Day Dah Light", which was recorded by Harry Belafonte as "Day O". Belafonte based his version on Miss Lou's recording.

She lectured extensively in the United States and the United Kingdom on Jamaican folklore and music and represented Jamaica all over the world. Her contribution to Jamaican culture is priceless and in 1974, she was awarded the Order of Jamaica and the government also appointed her Cultural Ambassador at Large for Jamaica. Among numerous other awards, she received the Institute of Jamaica's Musgrave Silver and Gold Medals for eminence in the field of Arts and Culture, the Norman Manley Award for Excellence (in the field of Arts), an Honorary Doctorate of Letters from the University of the West Indies (1983), and an Honorary Doctorate of Letters from York University, Toronto. On Jamaica's Independence Day in 2001, Miss Lou was awarded the Jamaican Order of Merit for her invaluable and distinguished contribution to the development of the Arts and Culture.

Snapshots of 50 years of achievements on the world stage

- Jamaica has consistently produced world class athletes, from the greatest sprinter ever, Usain Bolt; to Courtney Walsh, first bowler to take 500 test wickets and one of only four bowlers ever to have bowled over 5000 overs in Test cricket; to Mike McCallum who won world titles in 3 weight divisions and boxing heavyweight champion Trevor Berbick, Jamaica has made an indelible mark on the world across several sporting disciplines, particularly in track & field where the prowess of our athletes is nothing short of incredible.
- Jamaica has made significant contributions to the world through music, introducing mento, ska, rocksteady, reggae and dancehall to music lovers all over the globe. The late great Bob Marley is one of the most popular musicians of all time, Jimmy Cliff is an icon, producers Sly & Robbie are legendary worldwide; singer Diana King and dancehall aces Shaggy, Shabba Ranks and Sean Paul have crossed over and sold millions of records worldwide.
- Jamaican women are among some of the world's most beautiful, and some of our beauties have been outstanding throughout the years. Jamaica has produced three Miss Worlds – Carole Crawford in 1963, Cindy Breakspeare in 1976, Lisa Hanna in 1993; and a first runner up in Miss Universe,

Mural of Jamaican athletes on Knutsford Boulevard in Kingston

Wall painting of Bob Marley

Jody-Anne Maxwell with her coach Rev. Glen Archer

Yendi Phillips, in 2010. They have also placed in the top ten of both competitions on several occasions including the 2012 Miss Jamaica World, Deanna Robins, at the competition's 62nd staging in China.

- A nation's greatest asset is its people and Jamaica has produced some incredible sons and daughters who have done great things, including Dr. Henry Lowe, a renowned scientist; Gordon "Butch" Stewart, hotel magnate and owner of one of the world's most recognizable brands; Veronica Campbell-Brown, whose stellar accomplishments on the track has brought her country medals and glory over the course of her storied career; Jody-Anne Maxwell who at age 12 topped the world in the Scripps Howard National Spelling Bee championship in 1998 and Colin Powell, a former United States Secretary of State and retired four star general of the United States Army.
- Jamaican literature is world renowned and the island has been the birthplace or home of many important writers. From Claude McKay, the first Jamaican writer to get international recognition, to Herbert George de Lisser, whose novel 'The White Witch of Rosehall' is an internationally known classic, to Olive Senior who won the Commonwealth Writers Prize for 'Arrival of the Snake Woman' in 1989 and 'Discerner of Hearts' in 1995 to Kei Miller whose debut novel 'The Same Earth' won the Una Marson Prize for Literature, the standard of excellence will continue as we embark on another fifty years.
- Jamaican has made huge strides in the fashion industry, producing supermodels

2012 Miss Universe Jamaica 1st runner-up Racquel Jones wearing an Uzuri gown.

A large scale replica of Edna Manley's iconic sculpture "Negro Aroused" on Downtown Kingston's waterfront.

such as Althea Laing, Kimberly Mais, Jaunel McKenzie, Nell Robinson, Orane Barrett and Jeneil Williams; designers like the internationally acclaimed furniture and jewelry designer Claire Requa; and fashion design duo Uzuri International who were invited to South Africa to outfit the 2008 Miss World contestants for the opening segment. Jamaicans have been and continue to make waves in the fashion industry.

- Jamaican art is renowned the world over and the likes of Edna Manley, known as the mother of Jamaican art; Mallica "Kapo" Reynolds, one of Jamaica's most profound self taught artists, whose painting 'Shining Spring' was chosen by the government of Jamaica as a wedding gift to be presented to Prince Charles and Lady Diana Spencer as an encompassing example of Jamaican art; and Barrington Watson, one of the most influential figures in art in independent Jamaica, are just a few of the many great artists that have called this great nation home.
- Jamaica has made significant contributions to the world through film from a variety of talented directors and producers. Some of these include Perry Henzell's 1972 cult classic 'The Harder They Come' starring reggae legend Jimmy Cliff; 1976's 'Smile Orange' which was based on the play by the late Trevor Rhone; 1993's 'Cool Runnings', loosely based on the true story of the Jamaican bobsled team's debut in the1988 Winter Olympics; 'Dancehall Queen' in 1997, an urban drama; the critically acclaimed 'Better Mus' Come' released in 2010 by Storm Saulter and 'Fire in Babylon', the 2010 documentary film about the record-breaking West Indies cricket team of the 70s and 80s, shot in Britain but

funded by a Jamaican production company. Jamaica is one of the world's most naturally attractive locations for filming. International filmmakers have been coming to the island since the early 1900s and Jamaica has been the location of the world famous Bond Films; 'Island in the Sun' with the beautiful Dorothy Dandridge and most recently 'Knight & Day' with Tom Cruise and Cameron Diaz. Jamaican actors and actresses like Paul Campbell, Sheryl Lee Ralph, Madge Sinclair, Charles Hyatt and Leonie Forbes (theatre) have had successful international careers.

Looking towards the future

As Jamaica embarks on the journey towards another fifty years and seeks to capitalize on its history and the changing tempo of a globalized, fast-paced world, we must adapt if we hope to surive. With Jamaica's 2030 vision as the guide, 'Jamaica a place to invest, raise families and live', and as we look forward to a progressive and successful future, so too, must we in this 'Jamaica 50 Edition' of Beautiful Jamaica, project the next 50 years of growth for this small but great nation.

New Christiana Development Road

Palisadoes shoreline protection taking shape

By concentrating on infrastructure, the previous government continued the expansion of highways, completing the St. Catherine to Clarendon leg, and paved the way for investment by the China Development Bank in the toll highway from Spanish Town to Ewarton, with construction to begin in 2013. When completed it will greatly reduce the driving time between Kingston to Montego Bay.

In 2008 the government started construction of the new Falmouth cruise ship pier. It was completed in 2011 and is able to accommodate the largest cruise vessels. As a result cruise passenger arrivals has grown exponentially. The port was awarded 'Port of Year for 2011' by Seatrade Europe Insider Cruise Award in Hamburg, Germany.

In expanding the Port of Kingston to facilitate the largest container vessels operated by CMA/CGM and ZIM, and planning the Fort Augusta dry dock development with the China Harbour Engineering Company (CHEC), the Maritime industry is now set to play a more meaningful role in our future development.

The phased expansion of the Kingston Container Terminal along with the Fort Augusta development to accept the Panamax vessels being built to traverse the expanded Panama Canal (to be opened in 2014), will allow for maximum utilization of Kingston Harbour; one of the seven largest and safest harbours in the world.

The expansion of the Bogue Road in Montego Bay, facilitates great ease of travel for locals and visitors alike. The construction of the Palisadoes shoreline protection and a two-lane highway, protects the harbour while allowing for easier access to the airport and for future investment in Port Royal. Opening up the waterfront and connecting the new four-lane bridge at Portmore, and clearing the way for the east coast highway into St. Thomas and Portland, creates opportunities for investment in this picturesque area including Monaco type casinos and the deveopment of Navy Island to complement the new Rio Grande Bridge, the longest bridge in Jamaica.

Jamaica has signed 'open skies' agreements which will enable visitors to fly from Africa and the Far East. The proposed expansion of the Ian Flemming Airport in St. Mary will accommodate larger aircraft from the region and elsewhere.

Investment in infrastructure is of paramount importance. Improvement in the physical and economic infrastructure such as air and sea ports, roads and telecommunications networks, have a positive impact on productivity, resulting in economic growth. High-quality infrastructure improves access to public services, reduces negative environmental effects and supports the sustainable use of natural resources.

With the developments in the Panama Canal expected to shift global trade from the Pacific Rim region to the Atlantic region, Jamaica is in a prime position to be a major manufacturing hub within the Caribbean and Central America. The country is ideally located for manufacturers seeking near shore markets and is poised to capitalize on the demand for goods and services in the Latin American region.

Construction on Rio Grande bridge opening up new opportunities

Vernamfield

"...Last but of the greatest logistical significance in the area of air transportation is the Vernamfield development..."

Excerpt from Budget Presentation 2011-2012 by Minister of Transport & Works Mike Henry CD

"...The final element in this cluster is the long discussed development of Vernamfield. The efforts of the previous Minister of Transport and Works in articulating the compelling value proposition of Vernamfield as a long haul air cargo and passenger terminal, as well as a maintenance and repair operations (MRO) must be acknowledged...the establishment of an aerospace training institute by private interest underscores the possibilities for this development."

Excerpt of presentation made to Parliament by the Minister of Industry, Investment and Commerce Anthony Hylton: June 20, 2012

With the investment in the rehabilitation of the sugar industry and the rehabilitation of the railway as well as the opportunities for massive development of the south coast for green tourism, Jamaica is poised for economic growth. The proposed development of Vernamfield in Clarendon has the potential to make Jamaica the hub for cargo and passengers from the Far East and Africa in transit to North, Central and South America.

With the new thrust in diversifying energy needs and building an energy port, the government knows that this must be supported by an educated population, which is manifested in the growth of tertiary education and a people thirsting for knowledge – in the confident hope that we will prioritize social development to match our economic growth.

Yes indeed! The future is Jamaica's to hold and with enlightened leadership; and investments already amounting to billions of US dollars, the country's future is as bright as a typical sunny Jamaican day.